KIVA PUBLI

PRIESTESS
⊕OF LEMURIA

New Earth Visionaries
Illuminating the Path Forward

PRIESTESS OF LEMURIA
NEW EARTH VISIONARIES
ILLUMINATING THE PATH
FORWARD

SHANNON VAN DEN BERG

ANNABELLE HART · CRYSTAL JACKSON · DAINA GARDINER ·
DENA MCFADDIN · JACKIE GRAVES · JUNIPER REINA
ZORAYA · KATHY ELLER · LILA SOFIYAH · MÁRCIA
DÁROMCK MERMA · MARSHA GUPTON KING · SAMONE
MARIE

KIVA
PUBLISHING

Copy Editing: Christy Carlson

Formatting: Lisa Curtis

Cover Design by Muse Designs

ISBN-13: 9798399923376

CONTENTS

INTRODUCTION

THIS BOOK IS A BEACON FOR THE DAWNING AGE.

It was co-created by 12 incredible visionary women who remember the way through our current transition. They have come together to share their hearts and embodiment of Lemurian codes.

Lemuria was an ancient civilization that existed in the Pacific Ocean thousands of years ago. Yes, it was left out of our modern history books - as are other large truths we are waking up to - but many walking the Earth today know in their bones it existed.

I've always found it interesting that it survived multiple cycles of evolution before almost disappearing completely. Noticed I said *almost*. The reason this book was called forth to be co-created now, is because Lemuria holds the keys to transitioning into our Golden Age.

Lemuria was heaven on earth. It was a beautiful community of sacredness, joy and interconnectedness - an earthy, real life utopia. There are remnants still found and able to be felt across many cultures and lineages including Hawaii, Polynesia, Australia, the Celtic and Rose Lineages and more.

Priestess of Lemuria tells the awakening stories of starseeds, record keepers, healers and visionaries anchoring the Golden Age.

These women are the magnified echos of cosmic origins and ancient civilizations who are here to awaken the deep rememberings and infinite possibilities to co-create the fertile timelines which lie before us.

They are the empaths, mystics, sacred rebels, wild women, mermaid shapeshifters, dragon mamas, witches, water priestesses and frequency keepers the ancestors foretold of.

They are sentinels of hope, love and sacred power that benefits all. They are the liminal space of creation between heaven and earth. They hold space for humanity to re-imagine inner and outer paradise that will be passed down through the generations as the Lemurian wisdom was for us.

Come take a journey with us.

In these pages you'll be guided by Lemurian Priestesses who lead with their rare and brave hearts to open your heart and deeply remember. You'll get a glimpse into their evolving heart-centered expressions of life and business, and innate knowingness that flourishes from their intricate relationships to the ancient ones, the stars and Mama Gaia.

I invite you to grab a cup of tea or coffee and read a chapter at a time. Soak it in, integrate, feel it. These are life-changing stories these brave authors have poured their hearts into and bared their souls within. After each chapter you'll find the About the Author page and how to work with them if you feel drawn to deepen your relationship with Lemuria and your inner priestess.

Before you turn the page and dive in, place both hands over your heart. Close your eyes and breathe in and then out a few times. Connect to these women who bring forth these potent heart codes for you to receive. Breathe into your heart and be present with each chapter. There is so much wisdom and illumination here for you.

Listen deeply. Be open to remembering. Ancient medicine is waiting to reunite with you through these pages.

With Love,

Shannon xx

THE RHYTHM OF THE HEART

ANNABELLE HART

Heart of Lemuria:

In the words of *Shannon Van Den Berg,* (and *myself*):

"I believe the echoes from the Priestesses of Lemuria are not fading, but in fact, emanating. We are being reminded that we are never alone, and that there are wealthy resources of support available for us, with every breath, and every step."

WHAT IS LEMURIA?

BEFORE DISCUSSING LEMURIA, LET'S FIRST BEGIN briefly with *Atlantis*.

Atlantis is perhaps more well known, and more readily accepted as having existed. Some of you may have heard of Atlantis through the Disney movie. Personally, my awareness, perception, connection, and remembrance of Atlantis is quite different to the film depiction. Perhaps others of you know it through your own learnings/rememberings also.

Many of us may come to find our connection with Lemuria through Atlantis. That's how it was for me, but because Lemuria is less recognised/accepted, there can be a lingering sense of doubt/disbelief, which calls one into deeper realms of learning/remembering to *trust* your innate wisdom to *validate* oneself, even without confirmation.

I believe this is a very *potent medicine* that Lemuria carries for us, even to this day. Many of us, perhaps women most notably, are seemingly trapped in an endless cycle of doubting and disbelieving in ourselves. Many are distinctly disconnected and dissociated from their innate wisdom, distrusting in their Higher Self, Heart, and Womb Wisdom, uncertain about their body's intelligence and intuitive guidance, second-guessing their instinctual knowing and intrinsic senses. I see this as the result of a culmination of disempowering experiences across eons of our existence, where the balance between men and women has been in disarray, *to say the least.*

Atlantis is portrayed as having been more masculine in its approach to everyday living and being. It was considered a more modern version of ancient civilisations, but unfortunately it turned rather *toxic* and quite destructive in its fall. Atlantis is a *whole other story,* perhaps for another day. I mention it though, mainly because, for various epochs in our existence, we've witnessed (and perhaps many of us experienced firsthand) the multitude of effects and the exponential havoc that toxicity can reap through our systems, our wellbeing, and the ways in which it ripples severely through our societies.

*This is one of so many reasons why I (personally and professionally) practice a holistic approach to wellness, with the essence of my offerings being infused with the notion of **"Liberate.***

Validate. Regulate.", so that you may live in an experience of equilibrium (within oneself, and with All that is).

Though there is much more I could share on Atlantis, for now, let's move our focus back to Lemuria. There are a wealth of recollections one could share about Lemuria, too! However, let's simply summarise below with some of the key learnings/rememberings from my experiences, thus far.

As you read through this, I invite you to be aware of your Body, Heart, Mind, and Soul responses. Receive what resonates for you, and release anything that may not ring true for you.

Please note: some of these insights have been sourced from the *Lemurian Leadership Initiation,* with Shannon Van Den Berg, much of which resonates with my own findings.

- Lemuria is known as an advanced ancient civilisation, that some say existed between 13,000–56,000 years ago and pre-dated Atlantis.
- The vibrant lands and water of Lemuria were believed to have been located in the Pacific Ocean, perhaps between Australia, South America, and Hawaii, perhaps near Easter Island.
- Lemuria also has a strong connection to *Mintakan*, which, in part, makes up some of the *Orion's Belt.*
  It carries a strong sense of home for me, and for those who feel connected to Lemuria.

- Some believe there are threads that weave the remembrance of Lemuria through the *Ley Lines/Song Lines* of this *Earth.*
- Not only was it a technologically advanced time, but also one where the *Divine Masculine* and *Divine Feminine* lived in harmony (within oneself and with All).
  *The Quecha refer to this as "**Ayni**" which essentially*

means: to live in reciprocity, right relationship within and with All that is.

- There was a deep reverence for the Sacredness of All Life, an awareness of the interconnectedness of all Beings.
- It was a bridge between worlds (between the Masculine-Mind and Feminine-Heart, between the Heavens above and Earth below, and far beyond into multi-dimensional realms).
- There was Royalty and Priestesses for all streams of life.
- The ancient art of rituals and ceremonies was revered, intrinsically woven through everyday life.
- Elemental Medicine was honoured through their intimate connection with Earth, Water, Fire, Air, and Ether.
  Oftentimes, this medicine is presented through the means of crystals and crystal grids, vortexes, and portals of healing (with the use of crystals, colour therapy, the Elements, multi-dimensional beings, and more), plants and Earth Medicines, stone temples, energy healing, etc.

- It was a time of collaboration and co-creation through the Highest Heart Integrity, intended to serve All.
- Some believe Lemuria has disappeared. Others say it was submerged into the Earth's core/depths of Her Oceans, and some perceive it journeyed into another dimension.
- With the falling/collapse/leaving of Lemuria, this brought through an immense grief and abandonment wounding, which, still to this day, is often so deeply embedded for so many of us that feel connected to this place (knowingly, or unknowingly), across time and space.
  Simply hearing the name of this book (while I was having a bath) brought full body tingles, and a swirl of tears streamed down my cheeks. I felt my heart cracking wide open, clearing the residue and debris of experiences that

lingered from long ago, and a softening as a deeper remembrance of Lemuria began anchoring in my heart.

I wonder if you noticed any stirrings from within, as you tuned in with the above?

If so, perhaps create a moment to allow all of this to assimilate at cellular and Soulful levels. Maybe bring one hand onto your heart, and one to your lower belly/womb. Simply hold yourself tenderly, and breathe intentionally, for a time. Allow any tears to stream freely, without judgment.

THE POWER OF PRANAYAMA

If you resonate with the essence of my offerings – supporting you to **"Liberate. Validate. Regulate."** – and if you find yourself living in a state of toxicity, which negatively affects your inner and outer well-being, and if you carry the weight of abandonment wounds, I am compelled to share this chapter with you. Together, let's explore the transformative potential of *self-regulating practices,* specifically delving into *The Power of Pranayama.* These practices can guide you towards inner harmony.

The Translation from *Sanskrit*:

- ***Pranayama*, meaning:**
Prana - life force, breath;

Yama - control, regulate.

I invite you to receive this moment as an opportunity to come home to your heart's natural rhythm, much like the ever-unfolding ebbs and flows of the ocean waves, rolling in and flowing out. As you soften and settle into this innate rhythm, you return to a space and state of heart coherence. It is within this rediscovery and reconnection to Your Inner Heart's Wisdom that one can truly live a fruitful and fulfilling existence.

Let's begin.

Become aware of your body. Notice how it feels.

- *Are there any aches and pains, or particular parts calling for your presence?*

If so, invite in a serene sense of gentleness and gratitude throughout your heart, giving thanks for this ability to *listen and honour your needs* in this moment, and all moments.

You may like to explore some gentle movements to help shift any stale or stagnant energy, allowing the day to simply wash away with every exhale.

Perhaps focalising these gentle movements with regards to the neck, shoulders, spine, and hips, or becoming aware of each body part from your crown to your toes, and allowing yourself to move intuitively.

Trust your body's innate wisdom.

Notice how you begin to settle deeper and deeper into stillness, as you release any previously held tension.

As the body begins to soothe itself, let's enhance this with the practice of conscious breathing.

Breathe in from the base of your belly, expanding through your lungs, and up to your chest; emanating the energy out through your crown.

Exhale from your chest, down through your lungs, and create a slight contraction of your lower belly to squeeze any stale and stagnant energy out through your roots.

Hold the intention with Mother Earth, asking for Her support in helping you to alchemise any *"Hucha"* (heavy) energy into *"Sami"* (light) energy.

Continue to consciously breathe with this expansive inhalation, and enriching exhalation.

Let's employ the practice of **Ujjayi Pranayama,** also known as **Oceanic Breathing or Victorious Breath.**

The Translation from *Sanskrit*:

- ***Ujjayi,* meaning:** Victory over
- ***Pranayama*** (as above)

Ujjayi Pranayama (breath regulating technique) is a powerful yogic practice that involves creating a soft, whispering sound through the throat during inhalation and exhalation. It's compared to the sound of the breeze dancing through the trees, or the ocean waves rolling into shore and flowing out again.

There are many benefits of practicing *Ujjayi Pranayama,* some of which include increasing lung capacity, improving focus and concentration, reducing stress and anxiety, creating a sense of calm and relaxation.

It is said that for the nine months that we are growing inside our mother's womb, during the gestation journey, we are listening to a sound that resembles the ocean waves. Hence, this is one of so many reasons why we are often deeply soothed when finding ourselves by the beach.

Ujjayi Pranayama can create a similar sound and soothing effect for the body. The vibrations of our inhalation and exhalation in this practice channel down the esophagus into a group of nerves called the *vagus nerve.* This is responsible for supporting so many of the body's innate functions and systems, and helps us soften into our *parasympathetic nervous system,* allowing us to *rest and digest* with ease and grace.

It's important to practice this technique slowly and mindfully, and to avoid straining or forcing the breath. With regular practice, you may find that *Ujjayi breath* becomes a powerful tool for cultivating inner peace and strength.

THE MECHANICS OF UJJAYI BREATH

With *Ujjayi* breath, you breathe in and out of the nose, with the lips sealed – no breath passes the lips. This also serves to build heat in the body, *supporting detoxification processes* in the body. The lips gently close, and although the breath is passing through the nostrils, the emphasis is in your throat. You create a constriction in the throat, as if breathing in and out of a thin straw.

Whilst maintaining a closed mouth position, be mindful of held tension in the teeth, jaw, throat, and/or neck – *let it go.* You can feel the breath stroke the back of your throat as you inhale, and exhale. This comes hand-in-hand with the audibility of the breath, compared often to the sound of ocean waves. The tone, the audibility, is smooth and steady, continuous, uninterrupted cycles of inhales and exhales. Often you cannot tell the difference in sound between the exchange of in and out breath cycles.

GUIDE TO PRACTICING UJJAYI PRANAYAMA

1. Find a comfortable seated or lying position with your spine straight, and shoulders relaxed.
   You can also practice Ujjayi breath during Yoga Asanas (poses) or other physical activities.

2. Begin by breathing in through your nose – from the base of your belly, filling your lungs, and expanding through your chest.

3. Exhale completely – from the chest, through the lungs, and down to the base of the belly.

4. On your next inhale, start to constrict the back of your throat slightly, as if you are trying to whisper.
   Intending to hear a soft hissing or whispering sound in the back of your throat.

5. As you continue to inhale deeply through your nose, try to make this sound louder and more distinct.
   Intending to feel the breath moving in and out of your throat, creating a sense of expansion and lengthening in your breath.

6. As you exhale, continue to make the same sound by constricting the back of your throat.
   Intending for the sound to be audible to yourself, but not necessarily to others around you.

7. Try to make your inhalation and exhalation smooth and even, with the same length and intensity.
   Intending for your breath to feel effortless and relaxed, despite the sound you are making.

8. Continue to practice *Ujjayi breath* for several minutes, focusing on the sound and rhythm of your breath.
   If your mind wanders, gently bring your attention back to your breath.

From here, we're further enhancing this practice of returning to our Heart's Natural Rhythm, by employing a *Heart Coherence Breathing/Meditation* practice, alongside and interwoven with *Ujjayi Pranayama.*

HEART COHERENCE BREATHING MEDITATION

Heart Coherence Breathing Meditation is a form of meditation that involves consciously regulating your breathing to create a state of coherence in your heart rhythm patterns. This practice can be done for just a few minutes each day, or for longer periods if desired. This state of coherence has been associated with increased emotional resilience and harmony, mental clarity, and physical well-being. Developing a consistent practice of *Heart Coherence Breathing Meditation* enhances all aspects of your well-being, and your ability to create a life you love.

GUIDE TO PRACTICING HEART COHERENCE BREATHING MEDITATION

- Following on from steps 1–3 previously outlined in **Guide to Practicing *Ujjayi* Pranayama,** ensure that you are in a quiet and comfortable place where you won't be disturbed.
- In addition, become aware of your roots connected with Mother Earth, and your crown connected with Father Sky.
- Close your eyes (if available to you now), or simply blink slowly and softly to start soothing oneself into deeper realms of stillness.
- Continue to inhale deeply, and exhale fully (with the use of *Ujjayi* Pranayama).

1. Place your hand over your heart, and focus your attention and awareness in the area of *Anahata Chakra* (Heart Centre).
   You can employ Anjali Mudra (direct translation is "Salutation Seal" or Prayer pose) by pressing the palms together, and anchoring the thumbs at the sternum, in the centre of your chest.

2. Inhale deeply for a count of five, filling your belly, lungs, and chest completely.

3. Hold your breath for a count of five.
    Be as present and relaxed as possible.

4. Exhale slowly for a count of five, allowing all the air to escape from your chest, lungs, and out of your belly.

5. Repeat this pattern of slowly and intimately inhaling, holding, and exhaling for several minutes, focusing your attention on your heart centre, and visualising or imagining a warm, glowing light emanating from this area.
    Feel this light expanding with each breath, and creating a sense of calm and coherence, spreading this essence throughout your body and Being.

6. With each inhale, imagine that you are drawing in pure love and light into *Anahata Chakra*. As you exhale, release any *"Hucha"* emotions or limiting beliefs that may be blocking you from fully connecting with your heart.

7. Imagine that your heart is a beautiful flower, opening, and blossoming, expanding with each breath.
    Feel the vastness and radiance of your heart with each passing moment.

8. As you continue to breathe in this way, make a sincere attempt to experience a regenerative feeling such as appreciation or care for someone or something in your life. Cultivating feelings of gratitude, compassion, *Munay* (the Quechua word for love), and *Metta* (which, in Theravada Buddhism, is a meditation focused on the development of unconditional love for all Beings).
    Try to re-experience the feeling you have for someone you love, a pet, a special place, an accomplishment, etc., or focus on a feeling of calm and ease. Then, imagine this

loving essence pulsating in and out from your heart, expanding to all that surrounds you and beyond.

From here, I invite you to dive deeper, and join me in my complimentary offering: a **Guided Meditation into the Heart of Lemuria.**

*You can access this complimentary offering by following my links, which you'll find in my "About The Author" section (which you'll find at the conclusion of my chapter).

WITH LOVE

Honestly, I feel we're only just getting started, and alas, one needs to close.

Essentially, from my own awareness, perceptions, connections, and experiences with regards to Lemuria (and the effects this particular epoch of existence has rippled at a cellular and Soulful level), I believe there is *potent medicine* on offer to be explored, in order to bring oneself into a space and state of equilibrium.

<u>This includes (and is not limited to):</u>

- Learning/remembering the importance of *"Liberate. Validate. Regulate."* and ways to support this notion.
- Dissolving the immense *Grief* carried in our hearts (and wombs- for women).
- Healing/integrating the wisdom from *Abandonment Wounding.*
- Learning/remembering to *TRUST* one's *Innate Wisdom.*
- Learning/remembering to live in *Ayni,* (right relationship/reciprocity).
- Returning to deep *reverence* for the Sacredness of all life, and honouring through the ancient arts of *Ritual/Ceremony.*
- Reconnecting with *Elemental Medicines.*

- Healing/integrating the wisdom from wounding around *Toxic Masculinity/Femininity.*
- Healing/integrating the wisdom from the *Core Wounds of Love.*
- Breaking through the *Barriers to Love.*
- Learning/remembering *Heart-Centred Leadership.*
- Embracing *Divine Union* within.
- Creating *bridges between "worlds."*
- Embracing *collaboration/co-creation.*
- Embodying *Royal Codes.*
- *And so it goes on.*

In closing, if any of the experiences or topics mentioned resonate with you, or if you sense a genuine curiosity to delve deeper, I extend my invitation for you to reach out, let's connect. It is an honour and privilege for me to accompany you on this transformative journey of self-discovery, and support you in rediscovering/reconnecting with the profound wisdom that resides within your innermost Being. Together, we can explore The Natural Rhythm of Your Heart, unveiling its innate guidance, and uncovering the path that leads to a more authentic and fulfilling existence. Let's embark on this epic journey together, wandering side by side towards a greater inner knowing of ourselves – the worlds within us, and around us.

ABOUT THE AUTHOR

ANNABELLE HART

Annabelle Hart is an International best-selling Author, Certified Children's Yoga Teacher, and Medicine Woman. Annabelle has an intimate knowing of the Soul-Mind-Body connection and shares a holistic approach to wellness. She facilitates unique Ceremonies, Retreats and Certified Courses designed to encourage "Liberation, Validation, and Regulation."

With over a decade of experiences and certified education, grounded in Shamanism, Sacred Sexuality/Union, Science, and Spirituality, Annabelle offers expansive techniques, empowering you to "Transform Traumas into Treasures," and live harmoniously. She interweaves Yoga (specialising with children/therapeutic practices), Ceremonial Cacao, Aromatherapy, Bach Flower Remedies, Crystal Sound Healing, Emotional Freedom Technique, Sacred Feminine Medicine Wheel, and more.

Annabelle loves exploring, learning languages, and experiencing cultures. She feels most alive dancing with Mother Earth or wandering among the wilderness and wonders of this world, and beyond. Annabelle enjoys expressing her creativity in the kitchen with Earth Medicines. She is a free-Spirited, open-minded, vibrant Being who is devoted to living passionately. Annabelle values wholesome connections, and enriching experiences.

Whether you're seeking to deepen your Spiritual presence, trust your inner wisdom/compass, or live more fruitfully, Annabelle is walking with you. Her compassionate presence creates a safe and Sacred space for you to explore, love, and evolve.

Follow the links below to connect and weave with Annabelle:

Linktr.ee: https://linktr.ee/annabellehart444
Facebook: https://www.facebook.com/bella.hart.9/
Instagram: https://www.instagram.com/annabelle_hart_/

MERKABIC JOURNEY

CRYSTAL JACKSON

WE ARE ON THE PRECIPICE OF GREAT CHANGE AND
many are feeling the timeline shifts in humanity. We are in our
next phase of evolution and the alchemical process of transforming
our society to elevated states of consciousness is well underway.
When I was channeling the message for this chapter what came
through is it is time to get in right relationship with self, Source,
others and all that is.

The merkaba symbol came into my awareness in connection
with this and this symbol represents the pathway to ascension to
the higher dimensions of the cosmos. It entails a higher-level
understanding of ourselves, life, and the planet. Merkabah is a
Hebrew word comprised of three words Mer-Ka-Ba. Mer can be
translated as light, Ka means spirit, and Ba refers to the body.
When these words are joined together it alludes to our body being
the vessel where our spirit can connect with divine light.

The merkaba symbol is about bringing into balance the opposing energies of dark and light, body and spirit, male and female, 3D and higher realms, and self with the divine. The Lemurians and other spiritually advanced societies understood this connection and could activate the merkabic field which allowed them to have a direct access point to the divine and experience prophetic visions, technological advances, and extraordinary insights.

SELF

We live in a society where we have largely disconnected from self, from the magic within and the miracles our physical vessel is capable of. There has been a lot of conditioning that makes us believe that the answers lie outside of ourselves which leads to us constantly seeking betterment through external forces. We continually have given our power away and it is now time to draw that power back into ourselves and become grounded within our own unique thread of consciousness. That requires being comfortable in our own vessels and having full trust that we have all the tools already within us.

That is not to say that we can't seek knowledge or guidance to navigate life or continue learning but to understand that those merely act as accelerators, and that the true power comes from within us. We can see the proof of this when two individuals are given the same knowledge and one has huge success from it and the other does not. Why is that? Typically, because the one acted on or fully embodied that knowledge while the other did not, thus showing how it is only by us tapping into our own power that things can actualize in our reality.

Many in our society have sacrificed self-care and nurturing our bodies appropriately in the pursuit of success. This is why we see so many seemingly successful people with a host of problems such as addictions, depression and poor health. I personally experienced this while I was working in corporate professions for nearly two decades. I was successfully managing multi-million-dollar businesses but I was stressed, tired, gaining weight and had started experiencing health issues. I was not happy, disempowered and stuck in a loop of patterns because I was not taking care of my vessel so I did not have access to anything different.

Our body is our divine vessel that allows us to ascend to our higher states of consciousness. We have to come back within our body in the stillness to gain clarity on what is right for us and then act from that place. When we take care of our physical body it clears out the gunk in our systems and allows us to have a clear channel to receive guidance from Source. This is the foundation, you cannot skip this part and expect to have long-term access to your gifts or states of higher consciousness. It must begin with self and then and only then can you move beyond it; if you try to circumvent this, you will find yourself being brought back here time and time again until you get in right relationship with your body.

SOURCE

God, Source, Universe and the Divine have been widely taught in our modern day as forces outside of ourselves that we need to physically go somewhere or be guided by a preacher, master or guru to fully access. What I have come to know as true is that while those things can help you connect if that feels aligned for you, you don't actually need those because each of us is already a divine thread of consciousness. We can access our own gateway to the divine through developing our spiritual connection and strengthening our direct portal to Source. There are many different ways or methods to do this and you just have to figure out which ones work best for you.

Lemurians understood this concept well and they utilized sacred geometry and crystal gridding to create pathways to connect to God. They understood the divinity that resides within us all and thus we are all co-creators in our world. Through their connection to Source they were able to alter their realities through almost instant manifestation. This required great personal responsibility in their thoughts, reactions and actions. They needed to ensure everything came from their heart space so that the manifestations would be born from love.

We have to remember that unlimited potential exists in the great mind. We are being asked to remember and nurture our individual connections to Source. You are an ember of spirit that can either slowly fade to ash or can be stoked into a vibrant flame. You are part of the story of our time and you are being called to co-create your world in union with the divine.

OTHERS

We are living in a world that encourages division, fear, self-centeredness and a scarcity mentality. Every week it seems like there is some new topic of conversation that is thrown our way causing people to pick sides. This is activating the dark parts of humanity's psyche and encouraging self-centered behaviors that harm others and further the conflict and separation in our world. This environment has led to abuse of power, hierarchies, manipulation and control tactics to keep people enslaved, and it is an environment that has been born out of insecurity and fear.

The thing is we are all interconnected so when we act from these lower frequencies it does not only affect those we aim it at, but the wound ripples out into humanity. The reverse is also true that the more of us who rise above or transmute these lower frequencies the greater the effect is on the whole. Understanding that these things we identify as bad such as greed, chaos and division are just lower expressions or shadows of the higher expressions of ascension, innocence and virtue. Once we understand that we then begin to realize that simply acknowledging, transmuting and elevating the frequency can change everything.

We are moving from the old paradigms of self-serving to whole serving, realizing that when we focus on the whole we can rest in the knowledge that we will all prosper as individuals within it. The ancient ascended civilizations realized this and had such innate wisdom and spirituality that there were no power struggles, only love and empowerment. They did not suffer with duality because everything was connected and was one. They were able to access the highest dimensions 11th and beyond whose essences are that of harmony, ultimate love, infinite knowledge, wisdom and oneness of all.

ALL THAT IS

"All that is" alludes to the idea that everything is evolving and connected including our human self, spirit, animals, plants, natural cycles and the universe. We are each a thread of unique consciousness that weaves into the cloth of our existence and the reality we know. Every single act or thought by anyone or thing carries a frequency that vibrates out and is experienced in the whole. This reminds us that we do matter and that our work and service in the world is felt well beyond what we can comprehend.

The Lemurians held the values of a belief in God (higher power) and love and respect for one another and the planet. They believed that they should spread this message and knowledge to as many people as possible so it could be stored within our DNA and preserved for future generations. There are many of us that are beginning to recall this information and lost technologies that have been lying dormant in our DNA. This remembrance does not always show up as actual information but can also be a deepening spiritual connection and inner wisdom.

They also stored this information in crystals that they took deep into the earth to preserve and store, these are known as Lemurian seed crystals. My belief is that storing these crystals in the earth imprinted these codes or frequencies within the ground itself—so not only can we connect to those crystals to tap into this knowledge but also into the ground or sacred sites that contain these frequencies. We are at a time when these echoes of information from the past are surfacing and that knowledge is shifting our collective consciousness.

MERKABA MEDITATION

I spoke in the beginning about the merkaba and the merkabic field so I wanted to include this meditation that will assist you in activating your merkaba. The merkaba connects us to our higher self, to feel unconditional love, manifest our reality and tap into other dimensions.

To begin, sit or lie down then take a few deep breaths.

Slowly imagine pulling white light or Chi through your soul star chakra then down the column activating each of the chakras: soul star, crown, third eye, throat, heart, solar plexus, sacral, root and earth star chakra. You should now see a column of light through your body connecting your soul star to your earth star chakra.

Take a few more deep breaths and expand that column outward, activating your entire auric field around your body.

Now we are going to activate the merkaba electromagnetic field. I want you to imagine a triangle or tetrahedron that begins at your knees and points upwards to several feet above your head, this is the male pyramid. Now imagine another pyramid or tetrahedron that begins at your shoulders and points downwards to several feet below your soles, this is the female pyramid.

Take a few more deep breaths anchoring in this electromagnetic field.

Next, imagine the male pyramid slowly beginning to spin counterclockwise or left to right. Then imagine the female pyramid slowly beginning to spin clockwise or right to left. Now imagine them continuing to spin faster in opposing directions.

Now visualize a center point between the two triangles and an expanding field of light coming from that point extending out past your body in an oval. Hold this visualization for at least 30 seconds. This may be difficult at first but you can extend the time you hold this visualization as you feel drawn and your concentration allows.

Now set an intention or vision for this session, thank the merkabic field for facilitating the connection to Source and say, "It is done."

Slowly pull yourself back into your aura and into the column of light going through your body and your chakras.

Take a few more deep grounding breaths. Feeling into your body, wiggle your fingers and your toes, move your neck side to side, and when you are ready open your eyes.

VISION OF THE FUTURE

What I see for the future is these ancient ascended ideals coming back and integrating into our society. A time when we love and accept others without feeling the need to influence or control their views or beliefs. When we can allow for our differences without fear. Celebrating one another's successes knowing there is more than enough for everyone.

The old patterns of scarcity, lack and tearing one another down in order to get ahead or make ourselves seem more important will be gone. The realization that we are all teachers or leaders of our own unique gifts and talents and no one is above another. That all of our unique perspectives, talents and voices are needed to continue the expansion and evolution of the human soul. That we will once again be able to tap into the highest dimensions and have a direct channel to source and all other intelligence on this timeline and beyond.

What is your vision for the future?

ABOUT THE AUTHOR

CRYSTAL JACKSON

Crystal Jackson is an International Best-Selling Author, Intuitive Business Synergist, Belief Disruptor and Dream Activator.

Crystal is passionate about helping women reclaim their personal power and become potent forces of change in the world we live. She supports her clients in creating soul-aligned businesses that are a subtle blend of strategy and soul while actualizing their dream lives of freedom, wealth and abundance.

She supports her clients through a process of deepening their intuition, belief reprogramming, emotional clearing, self-mastery and shadow work helping them to expand into higher levels of consciousness.

Facebook profile: https://www.facebook.com/crystal.gayle.j

Instagram: https://www.instagram.com/crystal.gayle.j/

Linktr.ee: https://linktr.ee/crystalgjackson

YOUR TRUEST HEALTH LIES WITHIN

DAINA GARDINER

"THAT AIN'T RIGHT…"

Years of scientific evidence and health advice suddenly became taboo.

Fear and confusion ran rampant throughout communities.

Illogical, unreasonable and completely contradicted messages about "the science."

Something deep within rumbled, my skepticism rising quickly.

COVID never did scare me. When I first heard about it, my husband and I were in Austria, enjoying Christmas markets and holiday goodies.

Surrounded by tourists, the last thing you'd think we'd want is to thrust ourselves into crowded Hapsburg castle tours or hustle with thousands of others for the next subway.

But we're not like most people…

WHEN THE COLLECTIVE COOKIE CRUMBLES

During my first Information Technology program, our project management class had small groups choose a project and list out all the steps to accomplish it.

Our group chose to strategize my move from Brandon Manitoba to Calgary Alberta, where I went to school.

As we listed all the stages of my relocation strategy, one guy piped up and said, "Well that won't work, you need to buy boxes from a storage facility." In fact, in my case, I simply chatted up the owner of the store beside my apartment and dropped in for boxes that were otherwise destined for the dumpster.

Yet this schoolmate argued that MY method of moving was all wrong!

That it would NEVER work!

Ya, dude, clearly I was wrong as I'm obviously stranded on the side of the highway with my free boxes full of stuff.

If the rules or message sounds silly or dumb, I will find a way to do it better!

Call it defiance. Call it curiosity. Call it whatever you want but this rule-bending streak led me to question everything about the so-called "pandemic" narrative.

And I began my own investigation into actual science, picking apart every single study or news article that media was shoving in the population's face. (I mean, if you're trying that hard, something's not right.)

Something inside me felt compelled to fight.

To stand up for what felt so very misaligned and corrupt.

Because, as Canada was being run by a raving lunatic, the narrative forced down our throats was falling apart at the seams.

Lies upon lies upon lies were piling up across the globe.

Yet so many were caught up in the deception that, astoundingly, so few were able to see the glaring breakdown of the "pandemic" message.

It begged the question… What made me see the tangled web of lies so clearly?

DECEIVE THEM, MAKE THEM FOLLOW

While I never feared the virus, I did fear the collective direction that people were heading in.

Why do intelligent, educated people suddenly stop asking questions about abrupt changes to logic or science?

Why did people turn into monsters and betray loved ones so readily?

Why do seemingly good people suddenly become obsessed with defaming a group based on something innocuous as their medical choices?

Lies.

Deception.

Strategy.

"Repeat a lie often enough and it becomes truth." Joseph Goebbels

Goebbels was Hitler's Propaganda Minister. Scouted for his

keen ability to use words to sway the public, Goebbels was immediately included in the Inner Circle of Hell. His words caused more damage and destruction across Europe than anything else because his words enabled everyone who fell for his bullshit to call out, vilify and ostracize their friends and neighbors.

How did a new strain of the flu become the world's worst nightmare for well over two years?

Lies and deception. And propaganda.

Appealing to fear, guilt, shame and scarcity.

Censorship of data that contradicts the narrative.

Repetition of a few key phrases and concepts.

Naming one group to vilify and blame for all the lockdowns, deaths, and job losses.

Just as those who stood up for friends and family, those who risked their lives to resist the Nazis, some of us continued to resist the propaganda over the past few years.

Again, what made us empower ourselves with knowledge rather than fall to the collective pressure to succumb to the nonsense?

Well, it's got to do with our intuitive connection to natural health.

THE DEMISE OF HEALTH UNDER MODERN MEDICINE

We've forgotten that our bodies are as natural as the trees, flowers, animals and earth around us.

Somehow, we've fallen for "quick fix" treatments to "heal" our ailments instead of looking for solutions.

Somehow people have stopped caring about their own health because it's simpler to pop a pill or accept that "it's in my genes."

How has this happened?

Propaganda.

This time from pharmaceutical companies and those agencies that regulate health care.

They appeal to emotions—exhaustion, fear, guilt, shame, pain and scarcity.

Advertisements for new drugs repeat a few key phrases that make people feel warm and fuzzy. Or give them hope.

Doctors stand on a pedestal and exude authority, regulating the data that they want you to hear.

It's not about health—it's about money.

And we've allowed the "quick fix" marketing propaganda to take away our power to heal naturally.

We're lied to, day after day.

Safe and effective…the biggest farce from the past few years.

It's so ingrained in our brains that we ignore when it's used within the same sentence as the deadly side effects or that it's not working at all!

ALL THE WRONG THINGS

I stood with my book club ladies, all of whom had taken the shot, except for me, and overheard one say, "Those who don't take the shot deserve to die!"

Oh, the humanity. The love. The peace, the caring, the

selflessness of taking the shot…

I proudly became a social pariah at that point.

My husband and I felt the ropes tightening and executed a complete emigration out of Canada in less than two months—sold or gave away all our stuff, sold our house and vehicles, and caught an airplane with four suitcases and two cats.

We fled Canada because our health mattered to us.

We moved to a community in Nicaragua where almost everyone lived life exactly as always. We met new people, crowded into restaurants with strangers, and shared food and drinks with new friends.

I think we both caught COVID but it was so incredibly mild and quick to get over that I almost didn't even register how I felt.

We did all the "wrong" things and somehow survived! And came out stronger, healthier and more educated than I ever imagined.

QUESTION EVERYTHING

I'm truly a skeptic at heart. I take each new angle of data far into a rabbit hole of information. It's truly a problem (or a gift).

COVID afforded thousands of opportunities to question the narrative because the propaganda had so many holes right from Day 1.

Canceling renowned immunologists and virologists for speaking up about their research? Wait…what?!?!

Citing medical law or politicians as viral experts? Laughable.

Stop taking vitamin D and other proven immune-building

nutrients? Um, nonsense.

That "pandemic" helped me consciously awaken to just how corrupt and devious our modern healthcare system is.

I mean, I knew that I'd been screwed over by modern medicine in my quest to find solutions for my Chronic Fatigue Syndrome, acne, ongoing digestive cramping, and more.

But to watch the government convene with Big Pharma and health conglomerates to acutely dupe the entire population was truly maddening. Yet fascinating.

I honestly feel like I grew exponentially—spiritually, intuitively, physically. Absolutely, I have had a lot of *"Ha! Told you so!"* moments, but tuning into my inner love, grace and curiosity keeps me grounded and more connected to the messages about my health that feel right for me.

It's what keeps me strong, healthy and radiant—MY soul and MY intuitive messages.

My vision is for women to stop blindly following Western medical advice that isn't personalized or aligned with what they truly feel or need.

And I am so ready to unleash the power of the feminine on the world to show just how magnificent we women can be when we do take back autonomy over our own health.

WHO YOU TRUST MATTERS: CHOOSE WISELY

Someone once said, you have to trust someone.

Is that true? What if that trust is enabling corruption and deceit? What if it's actively harming the health of humanity? What if that trust fails to open up the opportunity to ask questions and examine the situation further?

No one should be trusted blindly just because they're an expert or in a position of leadership. And people who tell you to trust them should always raise a red flag.

We, as a collective, need to stand up against Western medicine. It certainly has a time and a place, of course, but it cannot continue to be considered the ONLY source of truth for health.

Every choice I made for my health throughout the "pandemic" came from trust…trust in myself.

I knew in my soul that if I allowed myself to be coerced into something 100% misaligned with how I know my body heals and thrives, I would only be feeding the rumbling of a deadly earthquake that simmered beneath the surface of humanity.

If that meant being called a racist, misogynist, and a wasteful eater by our tyrannical dictator, hey, it's just more lies.

There has always been more than enough evidence floating around from intelligent, renowned experts that I felt absolutely comfortable standing my ground.

I've been true to MY body and my health and that's what shimmers and shines within me, enabling me to help other women tune into their best health.

To help guide them to release health care that doesn't work and embrace a more holistic, feminine strategy that propels them towards higher energy and magnificent health.

HEALTH IS PERSONAL RESPONSIBILITY

Humans today accept that the illnesses passed down by ancestors are just going to be inevitable problems we each have to deal with.

Poor health is blamed on DNA, on toxins, on nature.

But in reality, poor health is more often related to the choices we make—what we eat, how we move, what responsibility we take to reduce toxins, disease and health problems.

In placing blame elsewhere, we give up our power.

Not only do we let the government decide what should go into OUR own bodies. But we also let health coaches, bloggers, self-professed experts tell us what diets to follow, detoxes to do, supplements to pop, and treatments to test.

People too quickly turn outward for health solutions, taking advice even when it doesn't feel right to them.

And in blindly following only the advice of external sources, we give up our power.

Health is not a pharmaceutical drug.

Nor is it a chemically-bound IV treatment.

It's not talk therapy, a fad diet plan, an exhaustive list of supplements, or "more sunshine and exercise" either.

Health is personal.

COURAGE TRIUMPHS OVER FEAR

Your body intrinsically knows how to heal. It's just waiting for you to take the reins.

Important messages like food cravings, aches and pains, inflammatory digestion, fatigue and weight gain have been considered problems to solve. Instead, what might happen if you took a step back and asked yourself why those symptoms arise?

The severity of viral infections is one big message written in neon across the sky, too!

Our immune systems are magnificent. When strong and healthy, immunity takes care of all the viruses, bacteria, cancer cells and so much more to keep you energized, strong and vibrant.

And it's so easy to please, when you pay attention to it.

For years my immune system was something I "boosted" if I felt a cold coming on; otherwise, I ignored it. Now I love it each day with the nutrients that help it thrive.

My clients are women with exhaustion—extreme fatigue, defeating tiredness, brain fog, adrenal alarm and burnout, feeling as though they're surviving and barely getting by.

These women are taught little about holistic immunity and its role in exhaustion.

Either they're diagnosed with Adrenal Fatigue (aka burnout) because they're busy, they're burning the candle at both ends, and they've come to the end of that wick. And they're sent off with a bag full of adaptogens and told to "stress less."

Or they've been hit by the BIG E after a viral infection. If they were lucky enough to find a competent doctor who ran the correct lab test, they may have been told it was Epstein Barr Virus. Or perhaps it's long-haul viral fatigue and treated solely with antivirals.

Conventional medical care doesn't know how to address long-term exhaustion, so women are given a protocol that's 100% symptom-suppression and 100% incomplete.

That was me once.

I caught pneumonia at age 12 and didn't get over that bone-crushing fatigue until I fixed it myself (holistically and naturally) when I was around 36.

I had to give up all my extracurricular sports and activities in school. I didn't pursue my dream career after high school. I barely had any friends through my 20s, and my career became the only thing I had enough focus and attention for.

I lived with a deep disgust for myself and my life. My body couldn't keep up with my dreams and desires. My brain would not cooperate for a big exam or professional certification program. I just felt stuck, stagnant and alone.

And every medical specialist I turned to told me the same thing: *There is nothing we can do for you. Just learn to live with it.*

For over 20 years, I merely survived. I couldn't do anything "normal" without painful fatigue getting in my way.

I remember one of the last movies I went to as I battled fatigue. It was an early show, beginning around 7 pm. I fell asleep so deeply that I woke up disoriented and drooling! My friends just laughed at me, but I recall thinking, O*kay shit, I can't even attend a movie, what is wrong with me???*

For years after that, I only went to afternoon movies. Usually alone.

In the summer before my 29th birthday, my mom wanted family photos. We gathered in our yard—my parents, brother and handsome Golden Retriever Simon—and a few dozen pictures were taken.

When my mom sent me a few of the pictures, I opened them up and felt sucker-punched. I looked awful. Not only was I thoroughly embarrassed by how fat I'd become over the years but I truly looked like death. Pale, white skin and dull, stringy hair. Even my eyes looked a little like my soul had left the building.

That wake-up call was the butt-kicking I needed to finally dig deeper into my fatigue. And I felt called to do that naturally and holistically.

As I progressively restored my energy, I realized that real health isn't about suppressing symptoms. It's rejuvenating the functionality of organs, tissues and cells so that you, as someone with big dreams and ambitions, get to enjoy life without popping pills, extra naps, or "coping" with your illnesses.

You get to eliminate them, even ones you've been told would be with you forever.

But it takes YOU tuning inward and learning to listen to what your legacy wants you to hear. And, of course, taking the aligned actions to support natural healing and total health.

RAISE YOUR CONSCIOUSNESS AND TUNE INWARDS FIRST

Today, I feel healthier than ever because I tune into what my lineage and intuition teach me. I listen, learn and stay open to its messages. I hold the power over my health and body.

And I will only ever truly trust in myself because it's my body, my intuition, and my life that matters when it comes to my health.

We need to stand up collectively and take back our healing power.

Especially as women.

We need to feel excited about changing the way we consider health and healing. We need more natural ways of reversing sickness, and we must embrace prevention and reversal over treatment.

For me, as a holistic nutrition consultant, food will always be the first natural healing concept to master. Autonomous health begins with food. Knowing the root causes of your health problems and knowing what nutrient gaps are behind those will guide your nutrition choices easily and effortlessly.

I feel that I was put on this planet to guide women to take back control of their health, to trust that healing starts from within. Your voice, your inner guidance, she's strong, she wants you to be healthy. You need to listen to her more often first before you take action.

MISTAKES WERE MADE BUT WE CAN TRIUMPH

The unfortunate truth is that many of the warnings brought forth by experts who truly understood the mechanisms of the shots were true.

The number of cases of COVID are 3X+ in people who have had at least two shots, and only skyrockets the more boosters are taken.

Deaths among the vaccinated are higher than anyone else. Symptoms of COVID are so much worse in those with the shot in their bodies.

Not to mention the horrendous side effects and medical problems.

Epstein Barr Virus is getting reactivated at an alarming rate. Extreme fatigue, neurological toxicity and inflammation, and hormonal imbalances and dysfunction are at the top of the list.

The inner guidance and skepticism that so many of us felt allowed us to rise above and help raise the vibration of the universe. We are here to bring love, passion, creativity, and pure potentiality so that others can learn and grow into their own powers too.

My mission has shifted vastly in the past year to not only help women tune into their intuition but to detox and eliminate as much of the damage from the shots as possible. I'm here to talk and support you if this is something you feel is triggering your exhaustion, aches and pains, brain fog, and other symptoms. As a woman, you deserve to be heard and lovingly guided down your true healing path naturally.

True health starts from within.

ABOUT THE AUTHOR

DAINA GARDINER

Daina is a Holistic Nutrition Consultant and owner of The Energized Woman. She supports and guides female leaders in becoming their most energized, intuitive selves in order to create the career, business and life of their dreams.

She is wildly passionate about dissolving medical gaslighting for women with chronic exhaustion, burnout and brain fog, and helping them step outside of mainstream treatments. Her mission is to empower women to return to the roots of natural healing through body autonomy and health intuition. After helping to transform the energetics of dozens of women, she's fully immersed in the damage that mainstream health and wellness fads do to a woman's body and healing potential.

Her VIP Experience prescribes food as medicine, and helps women reclaim natural energy production with cyclical energetics for the female body. Having spent years living with chronic fatigue and eliminating her health problems naturally, Daina is devoted to rebalancing and restoring the health of each client's whole body so that they can live freely, energized and excited for life.

Daina lives with her husband and two cats in Nicaragua. She hopes to travel the world and embrace many new experiences before settling down in her perfect long-term home.

3 Ingredients for Fiercely Feminine Energy - Free Guide: https://www.theenergizedwoman.com/energy-hormones

Root Cause Deep Dive Discovery Consultation: https://www.theenergizedwoman.com/book

Other ways you can find Daina:

Insta @the.energized.woman

Tik Tok @the.energized.woman

www.theenergizedwoman.com

THE CALL OF THE LIGHTWORKER

DENA MCFADDIN

THE WATERS ARE CRYSTAL CLEAR, THE SMELL OF SEA
and sand fresh and vibrant, and my dragon sits beside me as we
take in the beauty that surrounds us and the energy of the waves. It
is so peaceful here, and the sun's rays are bringing light codes for
me to decipher at a later time. It is time to begin training the new
Lightworkers again. I call Arwyn to bend down so I can grasp the
harness and pull myself into the rider's seat. As we ascend into the
sky, I ask Spirit for grace and strength to complete this mission.
This group is exuberant, high energy and chomping at the bit for
this next lesson. I know which students I will need to encourage
and those I will need to reign in. I smile to myself as I see the
group in the open field below and gather my own energy in
preparation for showing them how to throw energy balls. And just
to get their attention, I send an energy ball into their midst as we
circle the group to land. Ah, memories of an old soul.

THE CALL

The calling came when I was much younger, but there was no one in my life to help guide me in the ways of the mystic. My grandparents were staunch Baptists so there was no enlightenment there, and my mother was simply trying to find her way in the world and take care of two children on her own. My brother and I spent our summers with our grandparents in the retirement park and loved every minute of it. Something I did frequently was to ride my grandma's three-wheeled bike around the park and stop to talk and sing to the moon—Grandma would have to come looking for me because I stopped and did not return in a timely manner. And there are other memories of climbing onto the roof of the house that my family lived in to stare at the full moon. I cried during these moments, but I had no idea at that time why I was crying. What I can tell you now is that I cried for the unknown, the beauty of something I didn't understand. And perhaps I cried because I was human and could not fly amongst the stars. My first revelation that there was something more out there.

As I sit here, searching for what else my spirit is calling me to write, it occurs to me that what I have is simply a human timeline, or experience, to share. For some, there is a specific event that prompts a spiritual awakening—but as I think of things now, it was more of a cumulation of experiences that sent me on my journey of true self-discovery. There were a few traumatic events in my younger years, but none that actually initiated my spiritual awakening. If anything, the events that happened in my younger years resulted in me very quickly growing up and tucking my inner child away for safekeeping. I became the responsible one, the caretaker, the protector of others. The question is…did the experiences push me into that role or was I actually born to fulfill that role? Dharma. It took me well into adulthood to find and integrate that inner child and to ensure that she was accepted, safe and loved, and to find my true path.

THE HISTORY OF ME

Growing up I didn't have a consistent father figure and Mom worked two jobs for many years to support my brother and me. We managed to survive the era of no seatbelts, getting spanked with a belt and being left alone to entertain ourselves. There were many other kids that had similar, or worse, upbringings than my brother and I, but I know beyond a shadow of a doubt that my mom did the best she could with what she had. At the end of the day, we were clothed, fed and loved. She did meet the love of her life when I was about seventeen, but my brother and I were already out of the house; and though he was not present during our younger years, he has been present since he met my mom and we both definitely consider him a father figure. I appreciate his presence in our lives, but the lack of consistent masculine guidance while I was growing up resulted in some poor choices on my part. I was not well equipped to understand boys/men and made some seriously shitty decisions. This human life really is about choices and consequences.

It always felt as though something was missing from my life and I spent a lot of time looking for that *something*. I made a series of bad decisions, dropped classes and finally ended up quitting high school at the end of my junior year. Then, much to my mother's dislike, I started dating a man fifteen years my senior, moved out from home and eventually landed a job and an apartment. This ended up being in a dysfunctional, abusive, codependent relationship with him for eleven years. I then made some poor choices that drastically changed the trajectory of my life. I cannot say my life was changed in a bad way, but at the time I started a downward spiral emotionally to the point of considering suicide. I stole money from the place I worked to get out of the relationship I was in. The theft was discovered, I was fired and after months of court dates being dragged out I received a felony conviction, spent two weeks in a county jail, and then was shipped off to Colorado Springs where I spent a year and a half in a community corrections program that is somewhat akin to a work release program. During that time, I worked and started taking some basic courses at the community college. One of the managers at work made the comment one day that she thought I would be a great nurse and should go to nursing school, and so I did. After a few years I got my nursing degree and off I went to heal as many people as I could.

There was still something missing from my life, and I spent several years with different churches trying to fill the void. It is interesting that most people want to liken God to a "father" figure and that is how they introduce Him, talk about Him. But as I mentioned above that kind of male guidance was missing from my early life and so I had a hard time making that connection. What I have since come to believe is that there is a higher power, a source of creation, but I do not assign a specific gender or name to it. In my interactions with others, I may refer to this higher power as God, Source, Spirit, the Divine, and even Goddess at times. I also believe in science in that I believe every object, humans included, vibrates at different speeds and frequencies, and that navigating this life is all about what we put out into the universe and what we attract back. Have you ever met up with someone that was down in the dumps and when you spent time with them your vibe lowered as well, and you were no longer as chipper as you were when you first met up with them? That's an example of vibrations or frequencies. That person's energy level disrupted yours. The path of the Lightworker is to recognize things like that and keep to a higher frequency, thereby influencing others and helping them to raise their own vibration.

If I have to pick a particular moment or time that prompted me to begin self-discovery, I would say it was getting divorced from my wife of twelve years. I was lost and didn't know who I really was. Too many years of being what others needed instead of being what I needed. So at the ripe age of forty-six, I started the journey of discovering and embracing *me*. It started with counseling to get my head on straight, but then I discovered someone online that was hosting a new moon ceremony. A whole different world opened before me, and I am forever grateful. Over the past five years, I learned about Lightworkers, light codes, Shamanic ways, inner child discovery, and integration and shadow work. There was much work that took place, and I am a better person for it. After exploring different paths, I discovered that I am a crystal packing, energy healing mystical Shaman and have embraced my gifts. And this is how I became the Lightworker that I am today. I don't call myself a "Healer" though because I don't actually heal people. What I do is help them find their own path and do their own healing.

I mentioned shadow work and let me tell you, shadow work is no joke. Shadow work is the process of exploring your dark side, or the parts of yourself that you don't like or don't want to see. It's the work of integrating your shadow into your conscious self, and it can be a very powerful tool for personal growth. This is when you find and acknowledge the real you, the good, the bad and the ugly. As painful as some of that work was, I loved it because I was set free from the limiting beliefs, guilt, shame and general feelings of unworthiness. And the most important thing you can do is to forgive yourself! YOU are your own worst enemy and need to get out of your own way. And before you get too excited, once you believe you have *arrived* and have cleared all your trauma... there will be more to clear. That's just how it works, and how we continue to evolve.

TOOLS FOR SUCCESS

I want to share a few things that I believe will help you as you start your journey and will be instrumental in helping you to process the changes that will be heading your way. One of the easiest and simplest things I encourage you to do is to meditate, meditate, meditate. I'm not talking about doing this for hours on end or even for an hour. I'm talking about doing it for 5–10 minutes. Personally, I like guided meditations because they help me to relax and focus all at the same time. Seems a little incongruent, but when I focus on the voice that is guiding me the mental imagery kicks in and I forget the to-do list rolling around in my head. Sometimes I see colors, shapes or shadows, and sometimes I don't see anything. I can tell you for certain though that I am more focused once I am done. Another thing I recommend is to keep a journal nearby, not only for when you meditate, but just in your general area so that you can jot down thoughts as they come. Sometimes Spirit shows me something but I'm in the middle of something at work and can't take the time to ruminate on it. So I've started putting notes in my phone so that when I get home I can refresh my memory and take a few moments to decipher what it means for me. And yet another very important practice to do regularly is to clear yourself of the energies you've picked up throughout the day. There are many ways this can be accomplished but two of my favorites are to smudge myself with a sage bundle or take a salt bath. The bath helps to relax the muscles and the saltwater rinses away the energies. As you explore these different methods for yourself you will find what works best for you.

I also HIGHLY encourage you to find like-minded people to explore with and learn from. After taking the time to do the inner soul work and becoming comfortable with who I have become and my gifts, I signed up for a dating app. The dating app followed me to Nevada on one of my work trips there and started showing me men in the area. I reached out to one in particular and we started talking. Turns out that he was on a similar spiritual journey, and we had a lot in common. We stumbled upon each other during the height of Covid when everything was shut down—so our first date was in the hotel lobby with hotel security watching us and masks covering our faces! How's that for a first date? We each have our own spiritual practices but have learned much from each other and have integrated some of our practices together to better serve our clients. He is my Druid and I am his Shaman, and together we continue to evolve. Please don't think that we are now perfect because we found our new paths. When I stub my toe I still curse! We are still humans having human experiences. But we are sharing the light and higher frequencies as much as possible with others and helping them find their next life phase.

One of the biggest pieces of advice I can give is to pay attention to the signs. You are not losing your mind, you are not crazy or delusional, and *yes* you are receiving messages! You may be getting glimpses of future events or flashbacks of past lives to remind you of where you've been and where you still need to go. Make no mistake though, that little voice inside your head is going to tell you that you are crazy and making up things. This is your ego talking, and it's afraid. There is more to this human existence than meets the eye, and your ego will do all it can to keep you from opening your spiritual eyes. There are also many other dimensions of existence and just because you can't physically see those other dimensions doesn't mean they aren't real. There is no perfect time to embark on your spiritual journey, and if you are thinking you have to get your life in order first before you begin, you will have already reincarnated and started over again before that happens. Ha!

You are needed—and it's time to wake up!

HEED THE CALL

Why have I shared the condensed Reader's Digest version of my life with you? Well, the fact that you are reading this book tells me that you know there is something more to our existence than what we see. And my job is to tell you it's not too late to start, no matter your age or circumstances, and to encourage you to just take that one step, the first step. Talk to someone, your BFF perhaps, and have an open conversation with them about your thoughts. Yes, it's possible they may think you're crazy, but they may also have the same questions and curiosities that you do. We are constantly evolving and learning and true spirituality is so much more accepted today than in the past and is differentiated from being "religious." So read the book, watch the video, and ask the questions. Research the different paths available to you and discover which one speaks to your soul. There are many paths, and it takes us all to share the light and to raise the frequencies of this planet we live upon. You will never regret taking that first step, but you will forever regret not taking action.

Does discovering your spiritual path mean that you won't make mistakes or that you will be all "love, light and everything nice?" Hell no! The urge to cuss someone out will still come up from time to time, or you'll feel impatience because something isn't going your way, and you will still be triggered by something/someone...but as you do the work, those moments become fewer and fewer and your responses will be different. You will no longer choose to match those lower vibrations or spend energy on something that doesn't serve your highest good. Things will still happen but how you react is what changes. It all comes back to choices. So quiet that ego voice that would have you stay stuck, heed the call and take action. We are here to help guide you and come out of that spiritual closet! It's time to lean in and to trust your visions and dreams.

I'm not going to lie, though, the spiritual path isn't necessarily an easy path. It's not sexy, uber Zen-like, pretty or even all love and light like some would have you believe. You will have to put in the work. You will be clearing generational karma, societal conditioning and old wounds, cutting energetic cords that keep you connected to people that no longer serve your highest good, and loving and re-integrating your inner child. There will be tears and snot bubbles, lots of them, and then there will be healing.

I am a child of the seventies and even though there was sex, drugs and rock and roll, there weren't many teachings I could access about the enlightened path. There are so many teachers out there now though. We are the current-day Shamans, Druids, Oracles and Sages—and we are here to help! Also there are now so many books and teachings that there's no excuse for not activating.

Whether it's the sea, the stars or the forests that call to and resonate with you, you need to explore those connections. You can remain in darkness and ignorance, or you can let your freak flag fly and show others the way. What the world needs is YOU! You, exactly how you are, no edits, no censorship… and there are others that need to see you, just as you are, so that they too can take that first step.

Insert chapter eight text here. Insert chapter eight text here. Insert chapter eight text here. Insert chapter eight text here. Insert chapter eight text here. Insert chapter eight text here. Insert chapter eight text here. Insert chapter eight text here. Insert chapter eight text here.

ABOUT THE AUTHOR

DENA MCFADDIN

Dena McFaddin is a multidimensional soul, international best-selling author, Crystal Healing Facilitator and Reiki Master.

She has been a Registered Nurse for 20+ years and spends her time traveling between Arizona and Nevada, evaluating healthcare facilities and providing education to nurses to ensure that patients receive the best care possible.

After wandering the wilderness for 40+ years, just as the Israelites did millennia ago, she started on the path of the Lightworker. She did not subsist on quail and manna from heaven though... instead she survived on life's experiences and lessons. She started on her spiritual journey in order to heal but then gained so much more! She is still a nurse by day but now she and her partner do what they can to help others find their path and discover their gifts.

She is co-creator of Amethyst Heart, LLC and, together with her partner, offers Holistic Services and products to help those on their self-discovery journeys. She can be found on her personal and business social media accounts sharing life stories, encouragement, products and just some down right silliness to lighten the energy.

Website: https://amethystheartllc.fws.store/

Linktr.ee: https://linktr.ee/vegastoilclothing

IG: https://www.instagram.com/amethystheartllc/?igshid=ZGUzMzM3NWJiOQ%3D%3D

TO ALL THE PRIESTESSES IN HIDING

JACKIE GRAVES

THE NEW DAWN IS BIRTHING.

You are the midwives, the healers, the leaders, the visionaries, the edge walkers, the magic carpet riders. You are the light.

We need you—and the time is now.

We need you to stand up and raise your voice. To stand up and be seen. To claim your gifts. To manifest your visions, dreams, and desires. To OWN the blessing that you are. To walk the path that only you can walk.

We need you NOW.

Yes, it takes courage to be the leader and the light—to look at the shadows others turn away from, to face your fear without flinching. But you can do it. You know you are fully supported. The divine has your back.

I know it hasn't felt safe in the past. We have been persecuted, hunted, stoned, and lynched. We have been outcast, shamed, cut down, and hanged.

They've tried to silence us.

And now our liberation demands that we speak up.

You are not alone—although I know sometimes you feel that you are.

You've dimmed your light in order to fit in. You've made yourself small to conform to the boxes of society, culture, and conditioning.

But now, a part of your soul is screaming:

I AM HERE!! Listen to ME!

You are awakening.

Yes, it feels scary.

It's a fragile thing—a tiny chick cracking out of its egg and coming to stand on shaky legs.

You are wobbly.

But you know your destiny is to fly.

You are here to be free—fully liberated—in this lifetime.

You are here to embody your magic.

You are here to know your power.

You are here to remember the goddess in you—the divine light that you are, uniquely created, and divinely called to share your gifts.

Welcome to your awakening.

The New Dawn is here.

In the 7th grade, I wrote a research report on the Salem Witch Trials. I made the cover page on a piece of yellow unlined paper, and carefully printed the title in alternating rainbow-colored markers. At the top of the page, I drew a tree with a noose hanging from it.

When I was 12, I was fascinated with magic. I devoured the stories of the girls "afflicted" by witchcraft, of Tituba, the Caribbean maid who told stories of magic, and the fervor that spread through Salem as girls accused each other to avoid being hanged themselves as witches.

I also knew that I wanted to be a writer every time I wrote stories in my journal.

Somehow the two were interconnected for me. It felt like magic when I wrote a poem. It felt like magic when I got lost for hours inside of books.

So many of us have heard old stories like the Salem Witch Trials. Women who went against cultural norms got labeled as witches and were burned at the stake. Intuitive, powerful, multidimensional women haven't felt safe to bring their magic out and let it be seen in the world.

Even the word "magic" is triggering for some.

My 79-year-old mom was raised Catholic and strongly conditioned that magic was wrong. To this day, she cringes when she hears me speak about being a priestess. She loves me, she wants to be supportive, but it's hard for her. It's the ultimate taboo, to speak of the divine feminine.

During the last several thousand years of patriarchal rule, women's roles have been sharply defined and limited. Women are so powerful; systems of control have sought to separate us from our bodies, shame us, condition us into believing that our intuition is crazy.

Our words are magical—they create our worlds. When we liberate our voices and come into alignment with our soul gifts, we are unstoppable. I know this book will help other women who are hiding their gifts, and who are ready to step out and lead in a new way—with love, and light and heart.

I'm so excited that I get to be a priestess who unapologetically shines her light and shares her gifts, and that I get to share this journey with you.

LIKE FALLING IN LOVE

You know when you're ALL IN, there is this quickening. The soul rises and speaks louder than the intellect. You surrender to the wild place inside and boldly step forward on the journey knowing you will say YES wherever the path may lead.

Like I knew my husband was for me before I even met him.

"You have to meet Michael Torres," my dean said. "He's our new hire in the Theater Arts Department." She was a radiant African American woman in a tailored purple skirt suit. "He's a lot like you—bursting with passion about creativity and social justice."

Her 8th floor corner office had walls of glass. I'd just been hired on the tenure track in the English Department at Laney College and was buzzing with excitement and new possibilities. I could see the quad out the window, where light streamed in. On her desk, a huge vase of fragrant stargazer lilies thrilled my nostrils with their delirious scent.

When she said his name, Michael Torres, the light got shimmery in her office. I mean, it literally shimmered. I could see molecules dancing. I felt dizzy and kind of giddy. Like stepping out of time. A déjà vu. Another dimension. A kid in playtime, imagining and dreaming.

I must meet this man, I thought.

Creating the New Earth is a little like the exhilaration of falling in love. Light shimmers, your heart ignites, hours go by in minutes, and the smallest moments keep you enchanted for days.

THE SOUL YEARNS TO SPEAK

I've been a soul voice activator for a long time—I just didn't always know it consciously.

I was deeply empathic, partly because I'd been so silenced in my childhood. I learned to watch carefully before speaking, to feel deeply into a space, to sense the dynamics and underlying tensions, to be prepared for conflict to explode and brace myself for it.

I spent my childhood walking on eggshells so I wouldn't be seen or heard. My father was a terrifying and silencing figure. I was convinced that in his rage he would kill my mom, my sisters, our dog, or me. Anything could set him off. A fork tine scraping the plate when my mom and sisters ate dinner in the kitchen, while he devoured his meal in the living room in front of the evening news. "Who's scraping the plate?" he'd hiss, and we'd all freeze, terrified he'd come stomping in with blazing eyes and an upturned palm.

Because of my sensitivity, I could see the TRUTH inside my students that they yearned to bring out, the stories they needed to tell. I could sense the stirrings of a soul awakening—and I derived so much joy from the lights turning on in my students' eyes. The moments of connection, the aha's, the healing. Learning is remembering, awakening to the wisdom that's inside of us, reflected in the outer world.

My first teaching experience was traumatic. The South Bronx in the early 1990s at the height of the crack epidemic. I had graduated from Williams College, a scholarship kid with my shiny *cum laude* Economics degree. I felt a calling to teach. Teach for America was in its first year—and 500 potential teachers who trained for a summer were thrust into underfunded schools with only a few weeks of preparation.

I felt overwhelmed and scared. My class had no books, no supplies, black wire-covered windows, and empty crack vials on the playground. Fights broke out in the hallways, on the staircase, in the back of the classroom. I'd dreamed of changing the world and inspiring the youth. I'd been a successful student, a valedictorian. I wanted to give back. But I was a miserable failure.

I bought journals for my third-grade students from a street vendor in New York. Hard-backed notebooks they could write their thoughts in. Their words seared into my heart, exactly as they wrote them.

"I do not like my block

is all they do is kill," wrote one student.

"You are my favorite teacher.

You are a shiny star in my eyes," wrote another.

I saw poetry and trauma, beauty and devastation. I loved them and hated myself for not being enough. I gave until I was sick and drained, and it still wasn't enough.

When I look back on that younger version of me, I have so much compassion for her courage and heart, her deep desire to serve, and commitment to bring her gifts to the places that needed them most, to hold the light in a very dark time.

Thirty years later, one of my first students from the South Bronx emailed me. I was living 3,000 miles across the country in Oakland, California, still serving in a predominantly black and brown community. She tracked me down because she never forgot me. She wrote: "You saw me when I thought I was invisible."

I would never forget her. I loved her fiercely.

I've spent 32 years as an educator, and the last 18 years as a college professor. I've taught literature, composition, critical thinking, creative writing. My classes are popular and fill up quickly. My students have published books, read their poems from stages, and used their writing to transform their lives. My students tell me, "I was always afraid to speak up in school, but in your class, I found the courage" and "You changed my life."

I feel so lucky and grateful to have made an impact doing meaningful work. But the academy values the rational, logical, research side of the brain. It hasn't always valued the creative spirit—and most definitely not the spiritual.

Stepping out with my spiritual gifts required a massive identity shift. I was a respected pillar of my community, I had tenure, job security, financial security, all the things. But I knew I was being called to do more in my life. It felt like a part of me was dying—and indeed a part of me was.

I wanted to write and publish my books that I'd been working on since grad school, but the workload of prepping, teaching classes, and grading papers drained me. After many years, I'd finally written a memoir and it was time to publish. But I couldn't summon the courage. The frightened child in me was still scared to reveal the family secrets of my upbringing—the trauma, the terror, the mental illness, the shame.

RECLAIMING MY MAGIC

Then I found energy healing.

In my first session, a past life with my dad emerged. So much got stirred up that charged me with exhilarating energy. In this past life, I was a shaman and a dancer in ancient Ghana. I healed people in my tribe and exalted fertility in the crops through sacred movement. I shivered and vibrated in divine devotional dance. My gifts were celebrated by my family and my tribe reaped bountiful harvests.

My father was chief of the tribe. I was astonished to learn that my father in that lifetime carried the same soul as my father from this lifetime. My father was very powerful, and people were frightened of him—he used both light and dark magic to protect our tribe. Against my will, he sold me away from my family, marrying me off to a man much older. I didn't love this man. I bore several children by him, and lived my days far away from my family in a community that didn't value my gifts. I was inflamed with rage towards my father—and I shut off my magical abilities.

In my first energy healing session, I liberated this aspect of myself and reclaimed my magic.

I became captivated with energy healing. I studied many healing modalities and went to many healers. More and more of my magical gifts turned on, and I stepped into my sacred service.

Quantum healing feels like pure magic—it's blissful and effortless.

I ground into the earth, connect with divine source, and call in the light. I see into my clients' energy field where their energy is blocked. We unravel stories that have stifled their expression and they return to a state of love, where their true gifts emerge. They begin to speak up with courage and confidence, to have clarity about their soul purpose, and emanate a light that is radiant and magnetic.

To step into your soul truth is to return home. My clients say they want to have the look they see in my eyes—the calm quiet certainty of inner peace. They say they want to speak like I do, authentically, courageously, powerfully.

But what they really want is to touch the depths of their own souls, to face their own shadows. To speak their truths and unleash their unique medicine in the world—bringing healing and liberation to the planet.

The time is now. It is truly possible and it is a joy to walk this path.

LEARNING TO SPEAK YOUR TRUTH

When you start to speak your truth, it may be messy for a little while. But if you're like me, you already know the part of you yearning to speak can't stay pent up any longer.

I think about the trembling part of me, the little girl inside who was terrified to disturb the peace because her voice might cause the ones she loved to die. I want to tell her: "It's going to be OK. You will survive. You silenced yourself because you had to. I forgive you. I will always love you. I'm always here for you. You are brave and courageous, brilliant and bright. One day, your voice will be your greatest gift and you will use it in service to the world to liberate others."

I think about the college professor in me who was afraid her colleagues might think she was crazy because she channeled wisdom from other realms. She was afraid her Christian community would think her sacrilegious for speaking about how Jesus came to her, said "Be the light," and ignited her with his healing hands. The woman who feared her students would no longer love her because she left to follow the calling of her soul.

I think about the writer in me who worried her literary community would think her stories about angels and spirit guides, past lives and future progressions, astral travel and ancestral activations discredited her literary talent. I think about the terrified woman who wanted to hide her gifts, and I'm so grateful I chose to love her instead. I think about all the people I have been able to heal and activate so that they could serve at a higher level, in a way that's more aligned with their hearts.

Why would I hide the lightworker shamanista priestess in me? Why hide the fact that instead of spending hundreds of thousands of dollars on surgeries, emergency fees, ambulances, and rehab, you could have a light healing session with me to rewire the neural pathways in your brain and avoid a stroke in the first place? By removing energetic blockages in your heart, you could stop having heart palpitations. By removing blocks to manifesting abundance, you could receive a divine income doing what you love and living your soul's purpose. Why would I hide that I help people actualize their unique gifts? That's why we're here. How magical and beautiful is that?

I am overjoyed at the magic I bring through and the miracles I manifest. It's taken me years of inner work, lifetimes of work, to bring my shadow to light and transmute my pain into power. Now, I help other people unlock their soul gifts and stand in their power, too.

LEMURIAN LIGHT BLESSING

When I see heaven on earth, I see a beautiful ecosystem. An ecosystem of harmony—where each one supports the other, easily, effortlessly, from the overflowing love in their heart. So filled up. So nourished. So replenished and happy. Doing exactly what they were created to do.

Just like the trees give out oxygen we breathe it in, exhaling carbon dioxide that the trees use for photosynthesis. If every single human was singing their soul song in the world, we would have heaven on earth. We wouldn't have wars, depression, and trauma. We'd be creating magic. We'd all be weaving our beautiful tapestry of life exactly as we want to live it.

The things we consider as problems and obstacles are just beautiful opportunities to grow spiritually. To expand and create something that's never been seen before. To enjoy and celebrate and feel gratitude as more opportunities come.

This light is cradled in my hands like a white-gold ball of sunshine.

These hands appear before you.

Anointing your third eye with light.

Feel this light travel down the central column of your spine.

Connecting you to Earth below and heaven above.

You breathe in.

This divine blessing.

This now moment.

Your Lemurian codes awaken.

You open to the divine presence that showers down upon you

Like a radiant waterfall glistening and glimmering,

Refreshing and exhilarating.

There is no separation.

You are one with it all.

We all are one.

Feel the delight.

Feel the joy.

The water of life flows.

Fill your cup with it—and let it flow over you.

Drink this blessed water.

Taste freedom on your lips.

Smile knowing this is yours to receive in this lifetime.

Any time you wish.

You see the Universal symphony.

Light births in everything. Even the shadows have light.

Every challenge, every struggle—yields light when held with love.

This is a story of grace.

And so, you create.

Priestess, Creatrix, Divine One,

what will you choose to create?

This is no time to shrink, to hide, to dim your light.

Priestess, it's time to shine.

ABOUT THE AUTHOR

JACKIE GRAVES

Jackie Graves is a High Priestess of the New Golden Age. She is a #1 international best-selling author, educator, and Soul Voice Activator. Jackie is the creator of "Liberated Voice" and "The Holy Grail Codes: The 7 Keys of Soul Liberation," her signature programs. She helps badass women leaders heal, empower, and activate their voices so they can step out and change the world.

Jackie activates women leaders to express and actualize their soul gifts, so they can magnetize the life they want. With multidimensional energy healing and activations, she guides women to their deepest edges, to fearlessly face the blocks to their self-expression, so they can speak their highest truth and make their greatest impact, while experiencing lives of bliss and joy.

As an educator for over 30 years, and professor of English and Creative Writing at Laney College for 18 years, she has helped thousands of students find their voices and transform their lives. She lives with her husband in Oakland, California where she blesses the waters of the San Francisco Bay and communes with the redwood trees.

Website: https://www.jackiegraves.com/

Facebook: https://www.facebook.com/jackie.graves.10

Email: jackie@jackiegraves.com

REWEAVING THE SACRED: UNDOING THE SPELL OF SEPARATION

JUNIPER REINA ZORAYA

LIFE IS CALLING YOU FORWARD.

She is asking for more of you. She is inviting you to dance, to weave, to play with all of creation.

It's time for anything standing in the way of you sharing your heart and soul with the world to fall away.

It's possible to move through life with joy, with bliss, with delight. Even through life's shittiest moments, it's possible to laugh at the cosmic joke of it all.

Most of us have been living our lives in a trance, an illusion—that we are somehow separate from each other and separate from the Divine.

The true medicine exists in our way of being, in our way of relating to ourselves and others, in our way of dancing through life.

...

I was a quiet, sensitive child who loved connecting with nature. I'd sing to the plants and talk with the animals. My father gave me the name "Dancing Flower."

When I'd question the oddness of how society was structured, I was told over and over that this is just how it is. No, there's nothing wrong here. Get used to it. The sad chorus of those who had abandoned their dreams and settled into the feeling of powerlessness of creating any change.

But I never stopped believing. I knew life was more magical than I was being told. And even though I took some hard knocks, that belief of radical social change and the power of magick and love to create a new reality for all beings on Planet Earth never left me.

When I was in my mid-20s sitting in my teachers' hut in the jungle in Peru, I had a moment of poignant, blissful clarity. There I was listening to my beloved teachers chant Vedic mantra over the sounds of day transitioning into night as eight of us prepared to journey into the spirit world under the loving care of grandmother ayahuasca. It was a moment of such grace and confirmation that I was exactly where I needed to be that my heart overflowed with joy. Anyone who had ever denied magick's existence just didn't know where to look. And so I giggled to myself in delight.

As I've deepened my trust in life, I've been able to open myself more and more to the never-ending stream of miracles and synchronicities.

I feel truly blessed to live life with an open heart in connection to the earth, my voice, and my ancestors.

I've learned how to saturate even the most challenging,

unpleasant aspects of life with bliss.

I've learned how to surrender to the greater plan and enjoy the ride.

Yes, I still experience fear and other human emotions. But now I treat them as portals to embodied power and wisdom. Life's challenges are moments of initiation that guide me home to my truth as an unstoppable force of unconditional love, a pillar of delight, and a lighthouse for the weary traveler.

MY FIRST JOURNEY INTO THE UNDERWORLD

I spent most of my life in deep suffering.

Yes, I'd pierce through the pain with joy and purpose on occasion, but my default orientation was that of anxiety, anger, separation, loneliness, and despair.

This pain is what put me on a long and endless quest of "seeking." Suffering is how I found myself deeply immersed in the world of the healing arts as a profession.

You see, there were glimpses of repressed memories that would arise in the background of my thoughts from time to time. "Am I making this all up?" "Am I crazy?" These thoughts chased me around, creating a strong and constant undercurrent of doubt in my field.

Throughout my long healing journey, I came to realize that I agreed to experience this trauma as part of the alchemical process that would transform me into the leader, teacher, and healer I came here to be. This realization brought me great peace and allowed me to approach seeking support and sharing the experience with less charge.

When I was four years old, I was left in the care of two young female babysitters and another child my age. After some time together, the older of the two girls invited us to play some fun games if we'd promise not to tell our parents. It was like a spell. Over and over. Promise not to tell your parents. Promise not to tell your parents. It's our secret. It'll be fun. Do you agree? Do you agree?

The other little boy and I were convinced to take off our clothes, given a rudimentary explanation of what sex was, and encouraged to play with each other.

Something in my being knew the fundamental wrongness of the situation. I was able to muster the courage to expose the secret even though I had agreed not to.

My mom was mortified. Somehow, the emotional intensity of the situation caused me to shut down my voice and splinter off a piece of my soul.

I retreated to a space in my mind where no one could reach me. No one even knew I was stuck there.

I adopted several beliefs that served to protect me for a time:

"I'm all alone."

"The only one I can count on is me."

"I can't trust anyone."

From a meta perspective, I understand the vicious cycle that would have a young girl understand how to create a scene with this level of power play. My healing journey began with forgiveness. Forgiveness for the older babysitter. Forgiveness for her abuser. Forgiveness for the younger babysitter who tried to speak up against the scenario but was shut down. Forgiveness for my parents for leaving me with these people.

I'm way past the point of blame. Blame keeps us anchored in the past and prevents us from experiencing the joy of this now moment. However, I did need to feel it fully to move through and heal.

Sometimes we fall into comparison. I know I did. The thought, "It could have been worse," does nothing for healing! Trauma is trauma. For true healing to occur, whatever arises must receive attention and love. We must give it the space to unravel in its own timing.

I'm fascinated by the impact of beliefs and the stories we tell ourselves. So often people are still operating from protective mechanisms, stories, and ways of being that they adopted in childhood in order to survive. More often than not, these beliefs are no longer necessary (and possibly even harmful) to their success and happiness as adults.

Our thoughts and words have the power to create our reality. Our most foundational beliefs are formed in the first seven years of life.

I began to operate from the fundamental belief that life was unsafe. This led to me interacting with a great deal of unsavory characters and putting myself in harmful situations.

I didn't have the intimacy and communication skills to lean into vulnerability and express what was taking place in my inner world. I didn't have the discernment to know whom I could trust to be a safe landing pad.

Unless we summon the courage to reveal what's hidden inside our own minds, no one can offer us feedback on a different way of being and relating with ourselves and the world.

RECLAIMING MY FEMININE ESSENCE

Early in life, I received the distorted program: as a woman, you can be either smart or sexy, but not both. I chose smart.

Growing up, I was bullied for being weird and for loving learning. School came easily to me. Probably due to my many past lives as a scholar.

Even though I played sports, I spent most of my time in my mind rather than in my body. Even swimming laps, my thoughts never ceased!

The world of academia, for the most part, encourages competition and individualism. This suited me well. I followed tracks that allowed me to continue to isolate in my own mind, although on some level I truly longed for connection, collaboration, and community.

My insecurity was so high that I couldn't believe I was loved and accepted in my friend group. I always felt like an outsider.

Art and journaling were my only escapes from my overactive mind. Painting was my meditation.

Because so many limitations were put on girls, I did not like being in a female body. Bleeding felt scary, inconvenient, and shameful. I was taller than everyone and developed terrible posture hunching in an attempt to appear less tall and to be more "attractive."

Vassar College was like Heaven for me after thirteen years in Texas. I was now celebrated for being my weird self. I was introduced to meditation and yoga. I spent time at a nearby Tibetan Buddhist Monastery, sat with my campus's Buddhist Sangha, and was delighted by traveling lecturers.

Even with all this expansion, I remained in the prison of my mind and deepened the grooves of my internalized capitalistic mindset and masculine hustle. I needed to prove myself and work hard.

Competition creates and reinforces the illusion of scarcity.

Hyper-independence is a trauma response.

My body physically could not handle the energetic buildup from the atrocities and painful global realities I was learning about as an International Studies major. I did not know how to discharge the intensity and, at the age of 23, underwent a liver biopsy. In Chinese Medicine, the liver stores anger, which I had in excess.

This was a pivotal moment. I was told to stop drinking alcohol and lose weight. Over the next year, I saved money and learned my first healing arts modality (Reiki). I then set out for India, where I spent five months studying yoga, meditation, and energy work.

Although I had more ancient tools at my disposal, I was still in deep suffering. My complex issues surrounding intimacy, communication, and relating would take many more years to resolve. Outside the ashram, I almost immediately fell back into addiction, toxic relationships, and self-abandonment.

In the fall of 2016, my abysmal choices in whom to relate with and nonexistent boundaries reached an all-time high. I was in a toxic, abusive relationship with a gaslighting narcissist and pregnant. My reality was extremely unpleasant. I almost poisoned myself, taking herbs without knowing what I was doing. In the end, I chose to have an abortion, a choice I never thought I'd have to make. It was extremely painful physically, mentally, and emotionally. Spiritually, I came to understand that some souls' contracts on this plane do not include fully incarnating.

Before this experience, I felt like a genderless alien in a woman's body. This experience anchored me in reality. I am a woman. I have a womb.

I began to study tantra and sacred sexuality. I started to perform belly dance and shamanic ritual theater. It was healing to return to artistry and explore creative collaborations.

I embarked on a three-year apprenticeship in hands-on womb work, ancestral healing, and the feminine temple arts. Dismantling the patriarchy from within takes time.

I started to unravel the sisterhood wound. The witch wound. The mother wound.

All these fucking wounds!!! Will it never end? Fucking merry-go-round of shadow purge and integration.

And then there were times where I became addicted to purging, addicted to being in the shadow realms, addicted to seeking out that which stood in the way of my liberation.

There was so much density and distortion to move through! And much of it was not from this lifetime. Sometimes it was ancestral. Other times collective.

I had to let my wild dark feminine be free. I had to look at what I'd rather not see, including the manipulative and abusive aspects within my own being.

It wasn't until I had a mentor who worked with me intimately for three months that I was able to finally learn boundaries and discernment.

Before our work together, I didn't understand that I could determine with clarity and exactness what I was and was not available for. That yes, even the thoughts, incoming messages, and situations could all be managed through the clarity of my intention and the fierceness of my will.

One of the teachings I share in my work are the three keys to liberation: (1) listen and lean in, (2) deepen and descend, and (3) protect and provide.

In order to relax into my absolutely delectable feminine lusciousness, I had to activate my inner masculine's ability to protect that which is precious (me).

To think how little I once valued myself…

It's a symptom of a bigger, more complex issue that is shifting as we speak. We are returning to a reality where woman is sacred, where all of life is sacred.

CHANNELING THE VOICES OF MY ANCESTORS

During my first experience with shamanic soul retrieval, I flew with a guardian angel to retrieve a stone in which I had stored part of my soul. When we found the stone, I intuitively picked it up and ate it. Like a hatching egg cracking open, blue light flooded through the cracks of the stone and filled my entire body. The next morning, I awoke feeling more complete, like a piece I didn't understand had been missing had been returned.

My father was adopted. Having only half the picture of my ancestry made the mystery of my origins extra intriguing to me.

Shortly after Standing Rock, I was at a gathering in South Dakota with Lakota elder Cheryl Angel and other water protectors to pray at sacred sites for safe, clean drinking water for future generations. I was in a conversation with a man named Big Wind from the Arapaho nation about ancestry. When I told him I didn't know anything about half my ancestry he told me, "You better get on it. It's important to know where we come from."

My dad and I had previously exhausted the logical route of tracing his parentage. The paper trail would disappear across state lines. He was born in Yonkers, NY and adopted in Connecticut. Seemingly out of the blue, my mom, who had been divorced from my dad for decades, suggested that my brother and I gift my dad a DNA test after seeing a Father's Day special advertised. The results eventually came back but felt extremely vague and unsatisfying.

The next year, I sat in circle with a woman who was learning to read the Akashic records. I spoke to my desire to connect with my father's mother—I felt that she was still alive. She shared images of Slavic grandmothers cheering me on, rooting for me, and also got the sense that my grandmother was still alive. A few months later, I said yes to an ancestral healing retreat over the Thanksgiving Holiday. I felt myself open a portal and make contact with my grandmother. Just a few weeks later, between Christmas and New Year's, my dad called me to share that there was a DNA match and that he was in communication with his half-sister and hoping to soon talk to his birth mom.

We now visit and talk on the phone. She sends my dad handmade cards every holiday.

Through family stories and DNA testing, I understand my ethnicity to be primarily German, Jewish, Portuguese, Spanish, South Central Slavic, Eastern European, Italian, French, Scandinavian, British Islander, Greek, Egyptian, and Punjabi with some more ancient roots in Gujarat, Sri Lanka, Bengal, the Americas, East Asia, and Africa.

There is another way of connecting with our ancestors. The spirit realm.

Your ancestors are your biggest fans! They act as guardians, guides, and wisdom keepers.

They are walking with you every step of the way. All you need to do is develop a practice of speaking and listening to them.

My favorite way to connect with my ancestors is to open the Akashic records, connect with my womb, and let my ancestral songs flow through me.

Opening up my voice has been a journey that I'm still deepening into. Swimming with dolphins and whales played a major role in speeding up the process. They won't stand for anything keeping you from play, connection, and fully liberated expression.

Chanting mantra has been a key component in my journey toward blissful liberation. Every Sunday, I sit in community here in Hawai'i to chant the Gayatri Mantra 108 times, which amplifies the radiance of divine light. Since deepening my mantra practice, I've noticed synchronicities and miracles expand exponentially in my life.

...

So how do we undo the spell of the separation?

You have a unique role to play in this sacred tapestry called life. One that only you can discover.

It is time to remember how to listen to the whispers of your soul and befriend the unknown.

Your attention is your most valuable resource.

To take back your power, gain control of your attention, your energy, your mana.

Direct it with intention.

Use the power of your word to create what you want to see in your life and in the world.

Back up your word with aligned action and cultivate powerful allies who want to see you thrive.

Do not waste any of your precious energy on that which is crumbling away. Unless, of course, it is to dance with glee on the ashes of that which was never in service to love.

...

Dragon Mother, Quan Yin, She of Miracles and Compassion comes to you now.

NAMO GUAN SHI YIN PUSA

Open your heart to receive her blessing and flowing waters.

Breathe in the unconditional love of the Divine Mother.

Breathe out. Sigh, sound, and shake. Release what's no longer yours to carry.

Call upon the fierce protective love of Durga and Kali Ma.

JAI MATA KALI

KALI DURGE MA

Allow all that isn't love to fall away.

OM NAMAHA SHIVAYA

You are sacred.

You are held.

Your medicine is needed.

Your voice matters.

I love you.

...

A guided journey into the arms of love:
https://www.reweavingthesacred.love/f/pol-gift

ABOUT THE AUTHOR

JUNIPER REINA ZORAYA

Juniper Reina Zoraya is an Ancient Soul Whisperer, Best-Selling International Author, and Dragon Mama/CEO of Reweaving the Sacred.

Juniper supports people of all genders to be in their divine dharma, trust life, and enjoy the ride.

She serves sensitive, magical beings who are here to be of service to humanity and Mother Earth. Her work is designed to help you unplug from false programming, cultivate lasting peace, and dance through life in joyful service deeply rooted in your authentic medicine.

Juniper is a Mirror of Truth and Fierce Compassionate Love who brings levity and play to the journey of soul liberation.

She supports people with intimacy, sexuality, communication, discernment, and boundaries through liberated expression (play, song, dance, movement) and ancient tools for shifting consciousness (mantra, meditation, breathwork).

Within Juniper, Kali Ma and the Mother of Dragons meet The Maiden's sweet qualities of innocent, joyful play.

Juniper lives on the Big Island of Hawai'i, where she sings, paints, and dances with the elements. She gives thanks daily for all that called her to this magical 'aina to create at the feet of Tutu Pele.

Juniper offers nature-based spiritual retreats, personal empowerment journeys, and online classes for your blissfully accelerated liberation.

Reweaving the Sacred: https://www.reweavingthesacred.love/pol

Work with me: https://linktr.ee/j.r.z

Connect with me:
https://www.facebook.com/shecanwadeinadropofdew

START LIVING—GROW INTO WHO YOU WANT TO BECOME

KATHY ELLER

MY LIFE WAS REFLECTING ALL THAT WASN'T SERVING my well-being anymore. My mind was chaotic. Swirling this way and that way, out of control. I had to make a big change. A major move. Removing myself from certain aspects of my life, of my daily living. My daily living was over-achieving at being someone that hoped to be included, cared for by outside forces.

Over the years this need to be everything to everyone else has been the cause of my self-doubt and lack of confidence. Needing to be accepted. Needing, always needing! Yearning to be important to someone else. This takes me back to being a lonely little girl. The home I grew up in was busy, there was bitterness living there. That little girl was drowning in loneliness. She had an eagerness to be noticed, to be loved. She was loved but from a distance. She was searching to be significant to someone. Enter my later years, and I was still searching.

Something has been stirring over the last few years. *Enough is enough* was a message that came to me. That message has led me to a new path. Some might call it selfish. I call it survival. My journey of self-awareness is what has led me to my new life's path. A new way of thinking--of being.

One of the biggest lessons I learned from my friend Mary and her horses, aka Field Healers, is to be present and accept what is going on right now. Change the story of what is going on right now. When I am feeling those thoughts of doubt and not being worthy, I put my hand up and say to myself out loud, "NOT - TO - DAY." Nope, today I will not go there. I am worthy, and I am loved.

Spiritually twisted is what I call this time of my life right now. I have headed into a calm mindset that has brought me to a spiritual place. Being in a quiet meditative state of mind when sitting alone or walking in nature. A major part of my transformation has been to let go of the clutter physically and internally. Journaling has been that tool to help me to set intentions. When you write down your dreams you are setting an intention to see change.

Well, the big change for me was a physical one. Our former home was sold, and my sister and I decluttered our stuff and moved to an island, a maritime island in fact. It was unanimous. The need to be by the water was what pulled us away from our old lives. Once our intentions were set, the move accelerated. Keeping our dream to ourselves helped to manifest the move. We allowed no outside opinions to make us doubt our decision to live a new lifestyle.

One day I declared to a friend my dream for life. That dream was to be close to the water's edge to pursue my writing and creativity. Verbally declaring my dream was the springboard for my next move. That heartwarming feeling has stayed with me— guided me along my merry way.

This time around I have arrived at a place of peace, joy, and gratitude for life. I am not in that place of grief, a place of being exhausted by living anymore. This is a new time. I have no desire to ever go back or pressure myself to plan my future. My state of mind is to be in the present. Enjoying what is flowing to me today. Today when I plan for something it will be for an adventurous trip. To plan my garden. I make the choice to plan my meals. I do not predict my future. I do allow myself the pleasure of remembering so many loving memories.

At this time in my life, I have decided to start living, stop searching for unconditional acceptance. Time to give myself a break. Time to open the door and say goodbye to a life that doesn't work for me, I'm not accepting less than my heart's happiness anymore. Today I live from my heart. Like my friend Mary told me, "We can be the creator of our own 'Peace' of Heaven here on Earth."

I'd like to share a couple thoughts with you. My hope for you, after you have read my chapter, is that you will return to being that Daydream Believer you once were. Right now, it is time for you to get busy *living* your life. These thoughts may help you to do just that.

STOP BLAMING EVERYONE ELSE FOR YOUR HEARTACHES

Let's come full circle in life. Let's rebirth ourselves. When we take ownership of our own heartache maybe then can we start a new life.

Your change isn't the responsibility of someone else. If we want to see change, we must make the choice to change our own circumstances. Taking the steps to fix our heartache isn't always the easiest road to take. First, we don't want to hurt anyone. Second, we have come to rely on certain people to help us live. Change is scary and can seem lonely, like a bird flying out of the nest. Flying away to begin its life. A single leap of faith, a single big step to emerge into a new life.

We are, by nature, community-minded beings. The fear of stepping out on our own is what holds us back. Finding a way to venture outward is something I will set an intention for. When you don't have the answers, set an intention out to the universe. In time, the answers will arrive. During this time, you will more than likely start to make the changes needed to lead you to a new life you desire to live. They will be small, unassuming changes, but they will happen.

You are the change maker. Manifest positive change, and it will find you. I know for me I have been making the intention to watch how I react, learning how to give the situation a moment or two before reacting. Is what is happening right now worthy of my energy to get upset? Will saying something just add fuel to the fire? This can be hard to discern because this trigger is the reason this change is coming up. Sometimes I feel stuck in the fear of the change that needs to occur.

Take the pressure off yourself. Change isn't always physical; it can be a mindset shift. Setting boundaries will help. Those boundaries, by the way, are for you to uphold, no one else. Have open conversations with people. Let them know where you stand. Communication is key. If someone offended you, let them know how they just spoke to you won't be accepted by you. If you must remove yourself from the situation, do so. This space will hopefully in turn let the other person reflect on their own actions. You take responsibility for your own reactions.

My fear was that of physical change. As I mentioned at the beginning of this chapter, I did make a physical change with a move. Removing myself from what wasn't serving my well-being had to happen. Now my indecision is with my sister. We are sisters, friends, and our worst enemies at the same time. For our sake, we must find balance living together or choose to live apart. Removing resentment is key to resolving our situation. This will require some hard work. The work has begun though. The move to live by the water and spending time walking on the beach has been the therapy we needed.

THE POWER OF A GREAT SMILE

How often do we downplay ourselves to fit in? I was finding myself diminishing who I was to fit in. Don't want to rock the boat. It's like you are from a different planet if you shine your light too brightly. So, much of my lack of self-confidence was about trying to fit in. At this moment in my life, I am finally accepting who I am. Bringing back the shine to my sparkle. This sparkle usually begins with a smile.

Now that I have made a big change in my life, my sparkle has made a comeback. Like Mary Oliver says, "We all have a hungry heart, and one of the things we hunger for is happiness. So as much as I possibly could, I stayed where I was happy." A big part of my current happiness is going outside to the beach collecting stones and the odd piece of sea glass. My new lifestyle.

I have come to believe that this world needs more sparkle, corny as that may sound. This big old world needs your smile. And it can be a rosy-lip-coloured smile. Go for it—stand out, be the messy weirdo—be the stand-alone gal if you must. Just the other day I was in line at the post office and a gentleman returned the smile that I sent him. It was so easy to exchange a smile. For sure we made each other's day.

My thought for you is to stay bright. Stop and give a thought to when you feel diminished by a relentless glare. Stop and tell yourself a different story about this moment. Maybe the glare is coming from admiration. The person wearing that glare might just be wishing she could shine like you.

I'm hoping that with my stories you too will stop hiding. Don't dim your shining light just to fit in. Please, don't wait so long in life to realize this. Like the saying goes: "What a great smile you have. You should wear it more often."

WRITING FROM A PLACE OF PEACE, JOY, AND GRATITUDE CAN BE A CHALLENGE

When I am cultivating a new chapter, I am in a growth spurt. Each of my published chapters reflects one of those growth spurts. Now I am growing into writing about the good. It can be challenging because we are so programmed to listen to the gloomy gnarly bits. There is a stigma around this topic of good. Just like the stigma around talking about faith. When I mention faith, I'm not reflecting on organized groups. My thoughts go to faith as having faith in the good. Are we ready to shift ourselves to having more faith in a spiritual sense? Has the world lost itself because we have fallen out of faith?

What would happen in our daily lives if we started trusting in faith and the good it can bring? If walking into a brick wall isn't for you anymore, how about turning yourself in a different direction? Open the gate to your garden of hope. You are only one decision away from a new start.

Looking for your life's next chapter? It all starts with making the choice to make a change. Set that intention today. Reaching this point in life is all about the journey, isn't it? Make the trip worthwhile. Eat the cake, walk on the beach, stay up late to watch the stars, spend the money on adventures. Experiences are a lifetime of memories.

I wanted to share a quote I remember seeing, not sure who said it by it goes like this:

"You look happier since you decided to let people lose you instead of begging them to choose you." I had to stop and read that over again. I hate to say it but it's true. The reason for moving away was the feeling of being left behind. Not feeling a part of anything.

The move had to happen to fix me. Life away from my old experience has been great. Starting to fill up again. Meeting new people. This time my mindset is different. My mindset is more about me and how I want to show up in this world for my own sake. Not to be that person that someone wants me to be for their sake. I have moved on. I have grown forward since the day I realized that there had to be more. I have been moving along this merry way ever since.

Important relationships have grown stronger out of the big move. A large part of that, I believe, is due to the shift in my thinking. I'm okay that I have chosen my free will to be at peace over the thought of showing up as someone I had to be for others.

DON'T FORGET TO PAY ATTENTION TO RIGHT NOW WHILE YOU ARE SEARCHING FOR YOUR LIFE'S PURPOSE

While we are searching for our life's purpose, we can often miss out on the present moment. Are you listening to the whispers? Those taps on your shoulders? They are telling you to be present. Don't rush your day planning for a future you aren't even aware of yet. Your life purpose could just be that of being present with the right now. Enjoy your surroundings especially in nature, being in your creative world, or even while at work.

Living for the future is just as harmful as living from the past. Be present. Enjoy every minute of the right here and now. When you sit and be still, you can set an intention such as asking for clarity on how you can eat healthier. Or set an intention to be more active.

Ask spirit or your higher self: "How would you like me to show up today?" Sit with that thought. You can also ask, "What can I do today that will guide me to more clarity on my intentions?" Take a break with some quiet time. Be mindful of your thoughts. Take the time to turn off outside interruptions such as phones, TV, etc. Pay attention to your thoughts, not those of other people. Get busy doing the things that make you forget to look at your phone.

Be kind to yourself. Listen to your thoughts. Listen to how your body is responding. Your body will tell you when you need to avoid something. Be mindful of you, and you alone. Change the story you are telling yourself. Get up and move about, this will help you refocus and redirect your thoughts. I can't remember the number of thoughts we have a day but it's a whole lot. Hopefully my suggestions will help guide you to a more meaningful today by reminding you to just be in the moment.

A thought in closing… So how do you mend a broken heart? You move away from what wasn't serving you anymore—whether that's physically, mentally or emotionally. Planting my garden of hope is how I will be spending a time such as this, what once were waves of dissatisfaction have become waves of gratification. I'm spending early morning time to just be. Be present.

At this time in my life, I am enjoying being me, silly at times, childlike, not worrying about what someone might think. Taking it all in. Enjoying new adventures. Getting busy doing more of the things that make me happy. Taking time to giggle more. Sharing my sparkle with the world. Is it time for you to start to set intentions for living a whole full life?

We all have knowledge and talents that represent a seed. Grow your garden of hope by exploring your thoughts. When you spend time musing about your day, you will be inclined to reflect and journal.

Take this time to venture into your own mind when you are out in nature or out for a walk around town. Writing down your thoughts stimulates you to grow and to learn about yourself. You will begin to grow and open your thoughts to new ways of thinking. You may just make the choice to make some changes in your life. To step out of your ordinary way of thinking. Creating a new way of life with new thoughts and dreams. Changing the stories of past events can guide you to making these changes. Start writing down those difficult and sometimes sensitive conversations you have with yourself. Seeing them on paper, reflect on your words. Your written words will bring your inner conversations to life.

Have you been thinking of creatively writing down your thoughts? Follow me on Instagram and Facebook (links are in my bio). My journey could help you overcome any fear you may have of exploring your journaling experience. Follow my writing journey at www.musingabout.ca/musings. My writing has led me to produce my own publication Musing About Stories to Live By. I created this publication to help us all live a life from a place of good. My thought was: wouldn't it be great to lead by example of how to live a good life by offering uplifting content and resourceful and useful information? Musing About has a collection of articles and stories from various writers. The first step is to make a choice. The choice to make a change and start loving your life. Your life is your medicine so get busy living it. This restart can happen right now.

Coming soon! Island Life Journaling Retreat and my online journaling community. Spend a couple of days here on the red sandy beaches of Prince Edward Island or learn to journal with me online. Are you ready to share your story? Join my multi-author project for Musing About stories to live by. Who knows what life path your journaling will take you on.

I have become a best-selling author with the book *Magdalene Rising: Feminine Leaders Guided by Her Fierce and Unconditional Wisdom.* My second published chapter was in the best-selling book Isis – Mother of Magic. My third submitted chapter was in another best-selling book Magdalene Codes. All published by KIVA Publishing. Priestess of Lemuria is my fourth collaboration with Kiva Publishing.

ABOUT THE AUTHOR

KATHY ELLER

Kathy Eller is the owner/creator of Musing About Stories to Live By

When Kathy created Musing About Stories to Live by, she was thinking of all you creative beings.

To create a space to be brave with expression, creativity showcased. A space to make the choice to create a better today.

Kathy's thought is "wouldn't it be great to lead by example on how to live a good life with uplifting content and resourceful and informative stories?" Look at your life as though it is your medicine. You have a presence about you. Listen to your internal guidance. It is guiding you to move forward.

Coming soon! **Island Life Journaling Retreat** and our online journaling community. Spend a couple of days here on the red sandy shores of Prince Edward Island or learn to journal with Kathy's online community membership. Join the multi-author project for Musing About Stories to Live By. Who knows what life path your journaling will take you on. Kathy's daily practice of journaling has brought her to new paths in her life. She has become a three-time best-selling author with Kiva Publishing. Get started today! Receive your FREE 5 Day Journal challenge.

www.musingabout.ca

https://www.facebook.com/musingabout.ca

https://www.instagram.com/kathys_musings/

THE FEMININE WAY: STEPPING INTO EMBODIED FEMININE LEADERSHIP

LILA SOFIYAH

I FEEL WE ARE ALL BORN OF BOTH STARDUST AND EARTH particles. Made equally from the expanses of the heavens and the depths of the earth. Both human and divine. Matter and Spirit. As above, so below, as within, so without. The merging of this remembrance is what makes us whole.

This life is a journey into discovery and remembrance.

A returning home to who we are.

Beyond the stories, the imprints, the conditioning.

All of it shapes us and our experience, as we courageously uncover who we truly are at the core of our being.

It has become clear on my path that I am here for the restoration of the Divine Feminine wisdom on the planet at this time—which, as a whole, feels like a huge mission and a lofty goal. Though I know I am not here alone, a part of the many souls who have incarnated at this time to bring balance back into the world.

We are here for the creation of a new way of being. Bridging the wisdom of the past with the consciousness of now, I am honoring my multidimensional and multifaceted nature that exists beyond this time and reality. For me, these roots go back through Venus and Lemuria.

When I first heard of Lemuria years ago, something awoke in me. A remembrance, a knowing. Even the word LEMURIA, felt so ancient and resonant. At the time there wasn't a lot of easily accessible information about Lemuria. Atlantis, yes, but Lemuria was much more hidden and mysterious.

I would have dreams both waking and sleeping of what felt to me like Lemuria. A land of high frequency guided by beauty and love. A place where we were able to communicate telepathically and feel each other's emotions viscerally. For many of us, that first incarnation from the stars onto Earth was here, seeding this frequency onto the planet.

When I started to connect deeper to this Lemurian lineage, I uncovered deep sadness. A tapping into a part of me that longed to go home. That didn't want to be here on earth. That didn't feel like she belonged. That got told she was overly sensitive and emotional. And didn't feel safe to be here. Perhaps you can relate?

When we see time as linear, we can get stuck in the past, present and future. Though when we can expand our version of reality and see life as multi-dimensional, then there is the potential to know that there are many different realities happening simultaneously.

Dance has been my deepest medicine and the place where everything makes sense. Remembrances of past lives and other embodiments come into my awareness. Realities dissolve and I dissolve and all that's left is me in my embodied essence. Taking me out of my mind and connecting me to spirit. Where there are no words, only deep presence. Where I meet with Mother/Father/God and know myself as whole and holy. Knowing I am ENOUGH just as I am. Knowing truly that I am HOME.

LUMINARIES OF LOVE

Sister, I'm calling you home to your womb-heart!

To walk the Path of Beauty and the Way of Love.

Guided by the wisdom of the divine feminine essence that lives within us.

In recent years there has been a rising of the divine feminine on the planet. The divine feminine principle is a way of living in alignment with nature, reawakening our intuition, a return to a heart-centered way of being and a return into balance with ourselves, each other, the earth and all beings.

The wisdom and teachings awakening within many to inspire a reclaiming of our sovereignty, encouraging us to embrace our sensuality, pave a path of embodied feminine leadership and balance our divine masculine and feminine within us.

We are being called to move through any layers of distortion and fear that have kept us separate. This weaving together of our true natures helps us to remember and wake up to the truth of who we are so we can be part of the rebirth of the Golden Age here on Earth.

We are leading the way as a guide for a world created in compassion, embodied in truth and led by love.

Supporting the rise and remembrance of yourself as sovereign, whole and holy.

THE LINEAGE OF THE ROSE

It has been said that Sisterhood of the Rose initiated through the planet Venus onto the planet in the time of Lemuria, carrying through the temple priestesses and mystery schools of Atlantis,

Ancient Sumeria, Egypt, the Middle East, Greece and onto the Celtic lands of Avalon and the Divine Feminine lineages. That 144 women held circles of 12, each with 12 sisters, to activate humanity through love and unlock the inner knowing or gnosis of their true soul's remembrance within their physical body.

Can you hear yourself being called back to this gnosis?

Can you feel these circles of women in your awareness calling you home?

Coming together to reawaken the ancient mysteries within us, the remembrance of the lineage of the Sisterhood of the Rose and restoration of the Sophia Christ consciousness.

Seeding a new way of embodying our feminine essence through the wisdom of Venus as a guide and ally, as we connect and deepen with her cycles.

An invitation to tend lovingly to the innate beauty within us all as sacred sisters weaving a new story.

Empowered, embodied, awakening ancient remembrance together.

COMING HOME TO MYSELF

We all have those moments in our life that are turning points or thresholds from one state of awareness to another.

In 2015, I arrived home from a six-month trip and after a few days I started feeling ill, dismissing it as jet lag or a little bug I picked up on my travels.

As the days went by, I started feeling worse. After emergency room visits and many tests without answers, I got my partner to drop me off at the emergency room for the third time.

When they tried to send me home, though, I refused. I could feel my body was shutting down and knew that I had to advocate for myself to get the support I needed.

I had reached a point where I couldn't eat, lay down or stand without immense amounts of pain. Listening to that knowing deep within me that something was seriously wrong, and I was not going to get better without help.

My perseverance paid off and it was revealed I had a serious infection that my body was fighting. I don't remember much after that, as when they realized how sick I was, I was put on morphine right away. The next day they did an ultrasound and it revealed a large abscess, and within an hour I was in an ambulance on the way to a larger hospital nearby.

After 10 long days in the hospital, I was free to go home. I felt so grateful to have had access to the care that I received, knowing in another time or another part of the world I may have died. This is not something I take lightly.

When I was finally released, I remember arriving home. It felt so surreal, as I sat outside by the pond in front of my home, tears started streaming down my face. Feeling the beauty of this life, of nature and the gift of being alive. Soaking in the bird sounds, the dragonflies, the sun, the breeze on my face.

As I sat in my frail state—alive, humbled and so grateful—I heard my inner voice ask, "What is really important?"

In that moment everything dropped away and all that was left was deep connection. Connection to my body temple and soul essence, connection to my family and loved ones, and connection to nature and spirit which to me were one and the same.

I realized that so much of what I had put importance on in my life didn't really matter. The things, the attainments, the achievements, the objects. When everything was stripped away, it was really quite simple, and in that moment something shifted in me.

Don't get me wrong, I still love pretty things and to feel valued. I still have goals and visions. I am guided by the path of beauty and am lit up and inspired by art, music and creativity. Though at the core, I realized that all the external comforts and expressions in my life were created by showing up in authenticity and truth from this place of deep connection.

Sometimes in our most challenging times come the greatest lessons and growth. It's these experiences that help to shape us and expand our capacity. To increase our ability for compassion for others suffering through our own direct experiences. I know this experience changed me and allowed me to see the world in a different way. To find my center and know unwaveringly that this wisdom would stay with me and guide me.

Now every time I question what I am doing, when I feel overwhelmed or confused or don't know what direction to go in, I come back to this question of what is really important. Breathing it in...the simplicity, the centering back in and letting the fullness of it expand through my being.

Knowing that the only way is through and to continue to trust the support that guides me through each experience, challenge, opportunity and moment.

Coming back into my body. Grounding my feet on the earth. Breathing into my womb and my heart. Listening to the sounds of nature. Connecting with my loved ones. Guided by the wisdom of my body, heart and soul.

This is my center and everything else comes from this place of connection that starts deep within.

THE PRIESTESS PATH

For 17 years (and many lifetimes) I have been on the Priestess Path.

Initiated through the lineages of the Isis Magdalene Rose by the Goddess herself.

I haven't always been comfortable calling myself a priestess.

It was a title that, for years, felt so terrifying to even connect or speak to, that held wounding and fear.

I would have recurring dreams of being chained and burned. Remembrances of the travesties that have happened throughout the ages to women for standing in their power and sharing their spiritual and healing gifts.

While it was uncomfortable, it was important to uncover these wounds and fears that lived in my DNA. To know that I was not alone and that many of us were doing the work to heal these stories of the past. Healing our ancestral lineages as well as paving the path for those yet to come.

The Priestess Path has regained strength, and many are finding their voice and purpose again. They are remembering themselves as a bridge between the physical and spiritual worlds, being guided by intuition and inner wisdom. They are reawakening their inner channel guided by the divine feminine wisdom of the Goddess—rising as leaders, mystics and creatrixes honoring the cycles of the earth, the seasons, the cosmos and the inner rhythms of our bodies.

Stepping onto the Priestess Path takes great courage and vulnerability.

It is a path in service to the divine, to humanity and to ourselves.

A deep calling into the depths of our soul.

A connection with our ancient lineages, mystery teachings and authentic voice.

To walk this path of the priestess is one that I honor with great reverence. And being a guide for others on this path brings so much purpose and joy to my life. Whether initiating women on the path of alchemy and sacred union through Kundalini Dance or through cyclical wisdom and feminine mystery teachings through the Venus Rose Mystery school, I love knowing there are many paths that lead us home.

To be the bridge and allow the fullness of our authentic expression to shine. To reclaim and remember the light that shines from within and illuminate the path for ourselves and each other to embody the radiance we are.

STEPPING INTO GREATER VISIBILITY

In 2020 all my work I shared was in person. I had made the leap into being self-employed six years before and had been making my living sharing Ecstatic Dance Journeys through Dance Temple, Cacao Ceremonies, Women's Retreats, Breathwork and the yearly Kundalini Dance Training, I co-facilitated. I was sharing work I loved, though I had been intuitively sensing that there was more that I was being called to expand into.

It had been under the surface for years, this calling of my soul to stretch myself out of my comfort zone. To bring forth the ideas constantly streaming through me, and instead of accumulating more notebooks full of ideas, I felt called to deepen into what wanted to birth through me. To create an outlet to step more fully onto my priestess path and serve as a guide and mentor for others.

I thought for years about creating online offerings, watching friends and people who inspired me as they developed their online programs. But there was always a reason why not. I didn't know enough. The tech is too hard. I needed help. There were already other people doing what I was doing and so on. And I loved being in person with people!

Then 2020 hit and in-person offerings were no longer possible. Suddenly, I was at a place where moving my work online was a necessity.

I hired coaches, took business courses, watched webinars and videos, and followed people and signed up for way too many free events. So much of what I learned was valuable though it became overwhelming and confusing to have so many differing approaches, ways to do business and strategies swimming around in my head.

It's been a practice of navigating this world as a sensitive person, doing my best to not get pulled into overwhelm, comparison, self-judgment and not feeling good enough. Many times it all felt too much and I wanted to run away. Maybe you can relate!

It's been humbling being shown my vulnerable places, and this insight has given me the opportunity to love, accept and have compassion for myself as a human. To trust in my own soul expression and know that there is a place for each one of us.

As I reflect back on the past 3 years, I can see all that has shifted both internally and externally. These subtle changes, the inner awareness as I land deeper into myself feels the most rewarding.

It's taken me many years to feel comfortable sharing my successes, holding a wound of not wanting to shine too bright or take up too much space. Even saying YES to writing this book!

It's been so easy to be a guide and cheerleader to inspire my friends and clients to shine their light and now I am learning to turn that towards myself too. Celebrating the leaps and baby steps that we take in saying yes to the call of our soul.

To move past the fear of being seen each day and step forward to share our magic and beauty with the world.

To dismantle old, outdated ways of being that aren't aligned with the highest expression of our soul.

To find places to co-create, collaborate, inspire and lift each other up, breaking free from competition and comparison.

Knowing that we are more powerful together.

THE PATH OF ECSTATIC EMBODIMENT

At a festival in 2006, I experienced my first Kundalini Awakening—and in that moment the entire direction of my life changed.

I still remember that feeling as I danced and felt this jolt of energy open and expand through my whole body. A sense of pure love and ecstatic bliss. A feeling of vitality and activation as my emotional body heightened beyond anything I had ever experienced.

The next day it happened again. As energy flooded my body, I felt a blast through my heart even more fully than the day before. I remember having a conscious knowing that this was what it felt like to feel truly alive. Something so profound shifted in me as I realized that all the answers lay within me and that I had infinite access to this power. I knew I needed to find out more about this practice and how to experience more of it.

It turned out Leyolah Antara, the creator of Kundalini Dance, was coming in a few months to share her first ever workshop in Canada. Many synchronistic events followed that kept aligning for me to be there and as soon as that first weekend was done, I knew I had found my path.

For years I attended every training and retreat and became a certified facilitator, which then led me into a support role as retreat organizer, co-facilitator and trainer.

Through these years I was tested, guided and liberated. Coming home to my true essence again and again. A beautiful gift of this work is that it reveals what has been hidden so that these shadow parts can be alchemized and unified back into love.

These opportunities showed me my true path as an embodied feminine leader and what it was to create spaces for the awakening of women's power, passion and purpose. To come home to themselves and their unique wisdom and to allow that to shine in the world.

This path has connected me with women that are still some of my dearest sisters in the world. A true sisterhood, we've created bonds through allowing our radiance, our wounds, our vulnerability and all of ourselves to be seen, witnessed and shared to reveal our true essence within.

Kundalini Dance has transformed me—body, mind, heart and soul.

To say this path is life-changing is an understatement. It truly is an evolutionary path of remembering and becoming.

It continues to be the foundation of all the work I share. A leadership path, a priestess alchemy path, and a way of being.

Are you ready to step into the path of the Priestess?

To listen to your inner intuition and deep inner knowing?

To remember yourself as the wisdom keeper honoring the cycles within and all around.

It would be my honor to journey down this path with you.

To welcome you into sisterhood.

To be a guide, support and ally.

Knowing that when we journey together, so much is possible!

ABOUT THE AUTHOR

LILA SOFIYAH

Lila is the founder of the Venus Rose Mystery School and guide of the Wild Woman Wisdom Community. She is a Venusian Rose Priestess, Divine Feminine Mentor and Cyclical Wisdom guide.

Lila's mission has led her on a path to remember and reclaim the divine feminine wisdom that has been lost and hidden and help others access this within them.
Guided through the wisdom of the Divine Mother and the Sophia Christ Consciousness, devoted to the path of beauty and the way of love.

She is dedicated to the re-awakening of our intuition, power and radiance so that we can rise and co-create new ways of being together.

Guiding & inspires women to attune and embody their multifaceted unique essence within, through connecting and aligning to the natural rhythms and cycles of our bodies, the earth and the cosmos so that they can share their magic, beauty, and wisdom with the world.

You can find her on Salt Spring Island, living in community with her beloved and cat, stewarding her home temple and sharing dance both locally and internationally, guiding deep journeys of remembrance and embodiment and priestessing an online community and sisterhood.
https://www.facebook.com/groups/965601213958834

Website: http://www.lilasofiyah.com/

Work with me: https://linktr.ee/anandalila

Facebook: https://www.facebook.com/lilalovebee

STELLA MARIS - MERMA MAGDALENE MERMAID OF THE SEA MARYS OF THE SEA - LEMURIAN WATER PRIESTESSES

MÁRCIA DÁROMCK MERMA

THE SPIRIT OF WATER IS CALLING US TO REMEMBER THE ancient ways. No wonder why we are so drawn to seas, rivers, waterfalls, wells and lakes. Water holds a feminine loving and exquisite quality. Water and sound are the beginning of life on Earth and Lemuria holds the codes of this ancient wisdom. Water is the womb of life, the memory keeper and wisdom transmitter. Through her priestesses she sings the secrets of the world to us.

We are the Priestesses of Lemuria, returning and remembering what it is like to hold Earth—and all the natural world—as sacred. Many women are awakening and remembering their priestesses' gifts. We are in need of Lemuria's ancient wisdom back into our consciousness, to activate our magic and re-enchant Earth again, so we can be more playful, root, commune with invisible forces, reclaim our dreaming time to balance our working time, and feel pleasure, abundance, health and a sense of belonging. We are returning to natural time and weaving a new web of life, as opposed to the inherited, mechanical, manmade matrix of past generations. It is time to call forth the voice of our wise elders and ancestors, who were Biomancers, oracles of earth magic, and understood about living in harmony with Earth and the cycles of life.

LAND OF MU - SACRED UNION MEETING OF FIRE AND WATER

Rano Kau is an ancient Lady. She has been here on Earth for a very long time, 2.5 million years to be precise. Once a volcano that emerged from the depths, she is the dragon birther of the Southwestern section of Rapa Nui, an island in the Pacific Ocean and a piece of ancient Lemurian lands, now called Easter Island. She has seen a lot pass. She is a timekeeper. Yet, time has been watching and transforming her as well. In the beginning, she was a channel for fire, lava and smoke. She had her time of erupting, holding fire and rivers of lava and being very wild and fiery. Eventually she stopped and became a crater and lagoon, a womb of deep waters. Legend has it that the lake doesn't have a bottom— that it reaches the very core of the Earth. The lagoon is a nest for life now. She was once a house of fire: active, bubbling, erupting. Now, the fire is dead and she became a house of water. Every volcano eventually will transform into waters as much as lava becomes new land, new Earth.

Alive as fire, Mama Rano Kau held no life within her, she was full of yang energy, expression, and potency. Her fire created no life, but possibility. Now, from her waters, life emerges. Her waters hold, bear and nest life. Such is the mystery of life and death, fire and water. Such is the wisdom of this ancient Lemurian mother.

A water Priestess myself, I met her during the renowned December Solstice of 2012, a point in time that marked a crossing of eras, of an old world dissolving, and a new one yet to be reborn. It was early morning when I landed on Easter Island. Orion and Sirius greeted me on the west as I descended the airplane's stairway. Venus had just risen in the east. It was almost dawn. The first place I was called to go visit was mama volcano. I did it for many days, chanting, drumming, singing and praying with her. Walked her wild ridge and danced in abandon under the sun. A Lakota drum painted with snake medicine symbols was made specifically for this journey. I had prepared for weeks, meditating daily with a twin clear quartz crystal about 1lb in weight, and a breathing practice to unite heaven and earth with love in my heart.

I knew Easter Island was important for Lemurians, this ancient and legendary civilization, known to live in unity, expressing a very deep love for all nature. The field of union between masculine and feminine is balanced in Lemuria as their society and energy embraced nurturing and unconditional love, harmony and peace. In Lemuria the heart was open. Our feminine crown and womb awakened. Like Magdalene, we were truly connected to Gaia, the elements, the rhythms and cycles of life on Earth. In short, we lived in Eden, in organic and magic time.

Holding the twin quartz crystal in my hands I prayed before offering it to Gaia and Lady Rano Kau. On Solstice Day, with a prayer and a kiss I launched the twin crystal to the depths of the crater. My prayer was very specific: I prayed for the return of Sacred Union and the balance of Feminine and Masculine on Earth.

Almost five years later, on the September Equinox of 2017, I was in Big Island, Hawaii, another Lemurian vortex, at the mouth of yet another ancient lady volcano. This time, a very active and fiery lady called Kilauea, home of Mother Pele. She is a live womb portal to the center of the Earth, the womb of Gaia, from where new land is being created as lava erupts from her like rainfall and then flows slowly until it reaches the ocean and merges with water, dissolving the old and carrying the new-dreams, creations and paradigms.

We were a group of initiates on the path of love and womb awakening. In silence, as the sun set and nights fell, we communed with Mama Pele and her soft, red glow, compassionate love. Both experiences with these ancient volcanic mothers stirred buried memories within me. Back in Brazil, I recall them whenever I go to my local beach and watch the volcanic Island nearby. Something deep awakened within me—and years later, a lineage of water priestesses mermaids in the Magdalene tradition of the Saint Marys of the Seas introduced themselves to me, during another powerful cosmic alignment.

SISTERHOOD OF THE ROSE – MAGDALENE LEMURIAN MERMAIDS & THE POWER OF SOUND

The priestesses of Lemuria were water priestesses. They were spiritual keepers of ancient wisdom, love, beauty, and union. According to lore, they weaved the Sisterhood of the Rose into being, spiraling from Sirius and Venus, and rooting into Earth.

Mermaids and Sirens, before being demonized by patriarchal culture, were considered mistresses and guardians of the sacred power of sound, who use these frequencies to alter reality, (en)chanting the world with the power to create life and love. They were water priestesses who were real women - and a lineage. Mary Magdalene was a mermaid priestess.

Since prehistoric times sound and music have been associated with the power to create, heal and connect. Sound has no barrier, It can make, break, and rearrange molecular structure, it travels and penetrates solids, liquids and gasses. It is produced in the physical, but we cannot see it, nor taste, touch, or smell it…but we can listen to and feel it. The waters (emotions) moved in us by a song opens portals of remembrance. Soothing sounds can put us in a state of belonging, harmonic resonance, and coherence, where we may experience the "sound of the spheres", celestial harmonic frequencies of our original vibration. This is exactly the medicine of Lemurian Priestesses.

THE GRAND CONJUNCTION OF JUPITER AND SATURN IN AQUARIUS DECEMBER SOLSTICE OF 2020

Eight years after my encounter with mama Rano Kau, on the day of the Grand Conjunction of Jupiter and Saturn in Aquarius, Stella Maris MerMa arrived.

It was during the pandemic and I was living on the beach for several months, communing with land, wind, skies and waters. I was deeply attuned to the wild, Mary Magdalene, Sophia, the Rosary and the mermaids. I see now I prepared for the encounter with Stella Maris for months. Ten days before, I started leading a Rosary praying circle at dawn, and opened a sisterhood called "We are all Magdalenes" on solstice day. A couple of weeks before, I offered a womb awakening Magdalene Priestess retreat. The retreat began with a campfire on the sand by the rocks on the beach. Once fire was invoked, we entered the ocean calling to the primordial water dragon by singing songs to spirit keepers of the feminine mysteries, asking for permission, blessing and guidance. I sang a song by the great harpist and sound priestess Ani Williams calling for the Magdalene spirit in the waters. The song incorporates the gnostic text "Thunder - the perfect mind", attributed to Isis, Magdalene and the womb itself and goes like this:

I am the honored one and the scorned

I am holy bride and not the whore

I am the first and the last

I am the one whom they call life

I was sent forth from the power of One

Look upon me now and banish me no more

You who have waited hear and see me now

See all beauty hear my song within

Mary is rising, she is rising, she is rising up

From the rivers, from the mountains,

She is rising from the sea

Stella Maris, Stella Maris

Star of the Sea

I am she who cried out and I was cast forth

Upon the face of Earth in the darkest hours

Now I come shining on the sea

From my cave I am awakening

I am the substance of all nature

I am the law of life and the lawless one

I am she whom you had scattered

And now you gather me together

Mary is rising, Venus is rising, she is rising up

Stella Maris, Stella Maris star of the sea

The day was challenging and full of emotional clearing. Conflicts with my (ex)partner (now my great friend M, the merman) abounded, to the point that we decided to take a break from each other and go to different sites: he went to the waterfall and I went to the ocean by myself.

It was late afternoon.

To get to the beach, I passed entrance Five on Mary Magdalene Street—yes, there is a street on my local beach called Mary Magdalene! This day was sunny with a clear sky and a golden blue light. I took a plunge into the ocean...and then,

Magic happened!

Floating with my belly up, legs and arms spread wide open, I felt like Da Vinci's Vitruvian Man, where the code of the number 5 is revealed. Associated with Venus, the original 5-petal wild rose (before they became hybridized into multiple petals), and the pentagram, Five is a symbol of the feminine and fertility: it is the number of stations on the rosary and on the womb medicine wheel and is connected to the 5 elements. In Roman numerals is V, which in its origin stands for vulva and the feminine shape made by the yoni between a woman's legs.

I floated for a while feeling my star shape. Seen from Saturn/Jupiter/Aquarius conjunction angle, I would appear as a five-pointed star floating and glowing on the blue water element of planet Earth. At this point, a transmission came through. I heard a whisper and spoke some words, to soon realize it was a poem, then a song taking shape, a mermaid Magdalene and Sophia song about sacred union, which I called Stella Maris MerMa. The name also came in resonance to a plant medicine spiritual work in the Daime lineage called Stars Seeds, created by my dearest friend Juhliana

Terra. My song is about the seeds of the stars of the sea, sophianic magic, and sacred union of water and crystal.

The Grand Conjunction was a time of sacred union and seeding new structures and paradigms. My teacher Seren Bertrand calls Lady Saturn as the great Initiator and Enchantress, and refers to her as the cosmic Magdalene witch. Saturn initiates us in new structures often taught through a dive into the underworld, constriction, restriction and boundaries. Jupiter is the expander, holder of good luck, fortune, success, and generosity. Conjunct together, less than 1 degree apart, they held the codes of a new time. It was the closest distance between them since 1623.

This transmission felt as if the sea waters were giving me permission to call and assist the embodiment of the Magdalene mermaid lineage and archetype, to renew the waters of life. Later, I realized the mermaid herself whispered the words and the melody to me. I felt her presence then and now understand she has been my companion for years. Stella Maris MerMa, the mermaid. MerMa, my womb spiritual name, received in meditation six years before made perfect sense now.

Stella Maris is Mary Isis Pelagia, ancient water goddess bearer of life who holds the Venus archetype on Earth. The starfish and the sea biscuit both have 5 segments on their body. Along with octopus, and the number 8, they hold venusian energy seeded in water, just as roses are venusian frequencies seeded on Earth. She told me how ancient they were and how they hold the keys and codes for our awakening, healing, and embodiment. Five elements: alchemy-transformation-wholeness-harmony-love. She spoke about sacred union between water, the feminine, and salt, structure and the masculine order.

After this encounter, all the emotional debris I was carrying suddenly cleared. When I got home, my partner gave me a very precious gift from nature: a log with a dragon shape, taken from the depths of the freshwater river and waterfall. My shaft, to affirm and claim my role on Earth as a water priestess.

Since then, I have channeled at least another five songs bringing forth the spirit of Magdalene, the rose, mermaids and ancient mother goddesses like Inanna, Asherah, Sophia, and Maryah, expressing the alchemical process I have gone through since falling in love with sound healing through kundalini yoga and the gong until I reached the voice of the sirens that sing along the beaches swinging the seas of life.

To crown these experiences— retreat, Rosary, transmission of Stella Maris on the Grand Conjunction Day, and the dragon shaft—I received a blue, five-pointed star necklace from Mar.ina, a dear mermaid friend, guardian of a magical land where our retreat took place. When I received the necklace I felt the Lemurian wink again, as days earlier I prayed a 5th century prayer Stella Maris on the beach while praying the Rosary.

Saturn entered Pisces in March 2023 marking a new moment: she is asking us to center, reduce inner and outer noise so we listen and attune to the new song of Gaia, letting go of what is no longer working to create a new template for our lives. As prophesied by the Cathars, worshippers of Sophia and Magdalene, in 700 years the laurel would turn green and they would return once again to live and teach the Way of Love. We are the laurel and the rebirth of the Cathars, as we remember and restore the Church of Love and Union again rooting it into our bodies and into the Earth.

WATER MAGIC

Now Lemurian Priestesses are awakening globally as their mermaid attribute is coming online again. Water priestesses are exceptional sound healers who create and alchemize through sound and water. They heal using their voice, their clapping, by stomping their feet, touch, and by playing an instrument. With sound they move emotions, open memories and the corridor of time, allowing tears to drop, laughs to be heard and the hearts to open.

I would love to offer some guidance on how to attune to your inner MerMa(id):

- MAKE TIME TO WATCH WAVES BREAKING AND LISTEN TO THE SOUND OF THE SEA
- The oceans hold a unique signature song that was crafted only for you, this is a particular melody that only you will listen to if you make time to commune with it. The Sea has a song for each and every one of us. We need to plunge into the sea with our knowing and restored memory activated.
- PLUNGE into natural water like a mermaid, be it on a beach, river, lake or a waterfall. Dance, relax and move in the water. The Lady awaits you.
- TAKE AN INTENTIONAL BATH AND SHOWER imagining you are in nature under a waterfall. Cleanse yourself with a splash of ocean water after showering. Bathe with water collected from sacred sites, rose and herbs.
- SAVE OCEAN WATER AND CREATE A WATER ALTAR – anoint yourself, place your hands on her, sing with her.
- DRINK WATER CEREMONIALLY – saying grace and blessing her.
- WATER YOUR PLANTS WITH PRESENCE AND DEVOTION
- DO A WATER AND LIBATION RITUAL ON YOUR BELOVED – make time to cherish water and use for devotion and lovemaking

MERMA(ID) MEDICINE – LEMURIAN KEYS FOR TRANSITIONING

- Sound healing
- Water healing
- Daily water ceremony/prayer: life is the altar. Every single action, thought, and feeling is recorded on your field and is an offering to the Great Mother
- Death doula and grieving work with Mary Magdalene and Ma'at
- Singing and movement

FINAL PRAYER AND BLESSING

Magdalene of the Waters

Mermaid

Healing of emotions

Wash your daughters' hearts with your sacred waters

Rock our wildest dreams in your oceanic lap, in the ebb and flow of your waves

Even those we don't have the courage to dream

Stella Maris, MerMa

Here we surrender our prayers to you, so our emotions are purified and gifted with the Ecstasy of your Love.

Queen of Waters, sacred womb, source of life and death

Open our springs, our fertile fountain filled with the nectar of nectars.

Makes us in waterfalls.

Teaches us to become the woman that you are

The beauty of sacred relationships

Assist us to anchor a true sacred union on Earth.

Mermaid of the Waters, lunar enchantment, solar power, stellar frequency

Unite our waters and fires, our heaven and earth

Root us, nourish us

Sow in us the seeds of Love, freedom and the pleasure of living

Inanna Rakhma! All is love!.

ABOUT THE AUTHOR

MÁRCIA DÁROMCK MERMA

Márcia Dáromck MerMa is a Sacred Weaver on the Way of Love, a Rose Magdalene Womb Mystic, Grail Mermaid Priestess, and a Spirit Keeper of the Feminine Mysteries. She has been dedicating her life to awakening, healing, embodying and restoring the ancient feminine frequency and pre-patriarchal ancestral wisdom and anchoring the return of Sacred Sexual Union. She has worked with hundreds of people facilitating healing and transformation with Mary Magdalene & Yeshua, sound healing, yoga, plant medicine and shamanic practices. She loves to sing and write Magdalene and Mermaid songs and poems.

Teacher, translator, and artist, a former research scientist in Biomaterials and Pediatric Dentistry, she had a spiritual awakening in 2009 which led her to a career transition. In 2017 she created the "Temple of the Feminine Arts", a space dedicated to the return of feminine wisdom with love, art, pleasure and respect, serving as a uterine space for healing, creation and awakening of men and women. She leads study groups, ceremonies, retreats, with the Grail Mermaid lineage with Mary Magdalene and Yeshua, Ma'at, Sophia, Inanna and Pele. She created the Menstrual Education project and is a faculty member of the University of Biomancy, a school of magic founded by Dr. Azra Bertrand uniting science and spirituality.

To book a ROSE MAGDALENE MERMAID BLESSING SESSION follow this link: https://calendly.com/mdaronch/magdaleneblessing?month=2023-06

Instagram: @marcia.merma

Facebook: https://www.facebook.com/marcia.daronch

WHERE WE BLOOM: A TALE OF INSPIRED ACTION

MARSHA GUPTON KING

AND IT JUST SO HAPPENED...

...that from January 22, 2023, to April 21, 2023, she found herself in the middle of a quandary.

You see everything she wanted began to manifest quickly and with ease, and she wasn't used to that. Months earlier she had moved to Medellin, Colombia with no job, no home, no close friends, and no family on the continent.

Utterly alone but certainly not afraid she traversed the city.

Within days she thought it would be a good idea to purchase a home because she wanted to begin her path to citizenship in the country that had beckoned her to return after only a two-week vacation earlier that same year.

During her first month's stay in a hostel-like shared space in an Airbnb called Casa Verde, she was fortunate enough to have booked the largest room with a balcony and, what she would soon learn to be, a magical manifestation hammock.

HAMMOCK SPRINGS

In the early days of July 2022, she attached the set of hammock springs that she had packed and brought along knowing that most hammocks did not typically come equipped that way. After gifting her previous woven hammock complete with its own set of springs to a friend of hers that took over her apartment in Playa Del Carmen, Mexico she purchased a fresh set for the future.

They were ready for new hammocks to support. She obliged and installed them on day one.

From that moment she often sat in the comfortable, bouncy hammock. She let her thoughts drift to better days. Not that her days were terrible. Hardly! Her days were filled with perfect temperatures, fresh fruit wheeled lovingly to her door by the neighborhood vendor, workouts, an increase in calories while on a reverse diet, business negotiations followed by nights out on the town. Plus she took the occasional day trip to various, fabulous fincas on the outskirts of Medellin.

Oh, no, her days weren't bad at all. They were quite pleasant. What was missing, though, was a sense of ownership. She felt it was time to put down roots.

So here she was, hammocking, awaiting a business acquisition to go through so that she would receive her bonus. That was how she was going to fund the purchase of her new home. She had so much to discover and learn but while she was in the hammock she didn't strive for anything. She simply ALLOWED.

UNFOLDING

She allowed it all to unfold. She knew the strong sensation in her solar plexus that had pulled her there rapidly and effortlessly was not leading her wrong. She knew that the overarching wellness she felt inside of her body, which was oozing outward making her aura glorious and bright, was not accidental. She felt it was all by design. She just KNEW what she knew, and she LET it all be.

In the magical manifesting hammock she would envision those better days. She let her mind wander with wonder what they might look like but more and most importantly, what they would feel like. After reading Dr. Joe Dispenza's books *Breaking the Habit of Being Yourself* and *Becoming Supernatural*, she knew that in the quantum realm everything she could imagine already existed.

It was all already hers. All she needed to DO—and this was the most important work—was to vibrationally align with a particular point in space and time. How was she going to do that?

TIMELINE SHIFTING

She rested. She relaxed. She fed herself nutritious meals. She meditated. Then in that comfortable state, she envisioned her life. Where it was and in which part of town? Who was there? How it looked, smelled, and felt. She held that image and sat swinging, weightless, feeling the gratitude of already having it all because, in an alternate timeline, it existed already and was all already hers.

She would swing late into the night with overwhelming, completely encompassing gratitude. With one foot hanging over the side of the hammock she would give herself a push and then relax deeply into the catch of the fabric wrapping gently and lovingly around her body. She would breathe deep cleansing breaths. She would giggle quietly at the discovery that everything was already prepared for her and that the Universe was planning a big reveal.

She would envision her new home. She mentally planned the mural for the wall in the living room. She could taste, smell, and feel the warm coffee brewing in the French press. She was fascinated by the look and feel of the rich blue dishes she had already chosen for the kitchen. She knew how it would feel to recline on the all-white couch in the living room, while she gazed over the balcony railing onto the climbing mountainscape. She would marvel at the scattered vertical apartment buildings reaching high into the puffy cloud-filled skies. She could hear the sounds of the native birds and barking dogs in the distance. She enjoyed the faint sounds of reggaeton in the distance from a party that just ended at 7:00 am.

She knew HOW her new existence would feel so she just LET it unfold gently in perfect timing to align her finances, energy levels, work demands, writing obligations, and travel schedule.

Rocking, swaying, dreaming, feeling, she set intentions with a deep sense of ease, support, and abundance. She rested her mind and her heart. This was not just a new beginning but also a fresh start in a way she had not even considered yet.

COCOONING

After one month in the large room with the fabulous magical manifesting hammock...the strangest thing happened. She prepared to move to another Airbnb in a different neighborhood in town so that she could explore a new area and have a different set of experiences. Yet, that was not meant to be.

The next Airbnb that she had booked ended up not being unavailable which caused her to return back to Casa Verde. She was glad to be back in the safety and familiarity of her temporary home; however, they no longer had the large room available with the magical manifesting hammock. They only had an extremely tiny room that was previously used as quarters for a housekeeper. Knowing that she had many major expenses approaching in the coming months and that she had several weeks of upcoming travel, she agreed to take the tiny room. It was surprisingly cozy and comfortable.

It was like a perfect cocoon before the unveiling of a beautiful butterfly because what happened just before the change of rooms was quite miraculous. She found and made an offer on her new home!

NESTING

Casa Cielo would be the name she would give her 29th-floor penthouse apartment with 180-degree views of the Aburra Valley and surrounding mountain peaks.

She made the offer immediately and negotiated the terms of the deal in her budding second language. The business acquisition deal had also been finalized and the determined start date would be August 8, 2022. The Lion's Gate Portal. (The Lion's Gate Portal is an annual astrological event on August 8. Many people believe it helps manifest your desires and is an excellent opportunity to get out of the way and let your dreams come true. It is a portal that opens between the constellations of Virgo and Leo, which are represented by two different constellations in the night sky. The portal represents the opportunity for manifestation and making things happen rapidly.)

Also, her health was taking a turn for the better because she had been dealing with lingering stomach issues from her time in Mexico during her first month in Medellin. Yet, the month had been spent in repair and preparation for many beautiful events to come.

COMPLETION

Over the next six months, she would close on the house, move in, and pay the balance in full, in cash, by December 8, 2022. She would transition all the acquired business necessary to release the bonus into her checking account in the 3D realm because she had been mentally moving that money in the ether from the comfort of her cradling hammock for 30 days prior.

She would furnish her home and pay for it all as she went. She would host parties with guests being new friends and collaborators she had just recently met in Medellin. She would travel back to the United States to visit family and manage personal items. She would continue her workouts three to four days per week. She would even finish writing her first solo book which she had been researching and planning for a little over a year. It would feel like she was in labor and birthing a baby. There would be excitement, fear, anticipation, moments of feeling like quitting, and moments of great momentum. But she would persevere.

GROUNDING

She would complete the application and receive her investment visa and cedula (Colombian ID) which is a pathway to a second passport and citizenship in Colombia in five years. She would continue to learn Spanish.

She would incorporate her business. She would take on private kizomba students and find a new dance partner with whom she could give kizomba classes in town. She didn't need the money but would charge a small fee so that the students would show up and take their learning seriously. She would come to find out that one private lesson student per month would cover the costs of her monthly expenses in her home since she didn't have a mortgage.

She would have a unique, one-of-a-kind mural art installation completed in her home by mid-September from a budding artist in Medellin who would become a friend and colleague.

She would have her birthday and Christmas Day alone in her home because it was exactly the way she wanted to spend those days.

She would begin writing morning pages as created by Julia Cameron and write a 197-page book in 55 days enabling herself to believe in the power and productivity of a simple 30–45-minute writing block per day.

She would construct 10 daily health habits for herself and rewrite them day after day in order to make them a permanent fixture in her daily routine to learn to manipulate energy. She would track her weight and food beginning in July 2022 through 2023 to learn more about herself and her emotional eating (or not eating) habits keeping her metabolism stuck. And she would discover the reason she had not been able to change her weight or gain substantial muscle growth over the past two years was because she had not been eating enough.

She would attract and enjoy one of the most amazing lovers she had ever met and have multiple week-long encounters with him. She would surrender completely and fully and realize true primal embodiment for perhaps the first time ever because of him.

She would encourage and inspire others with her positivity, manifesting journey, and techniques. She would be invited to share more of this process with groups of Goddesses in Playa Del Carmen, Mexico in May 2023.

A FRESH HAMMOCK

She would have a steel structure frame manufactured to fit her balcony in Casa Cielo and installed to support a fresh new magical manifesting hammock equipped with the springs to make that hammock a light, bouncy, supportive space to allow more magical manifestations to well, you guessed it, manifest.

She would prepare for fresh sessions in the brand-new hammock, where she would envision, dream of, and feel into the next exciting and exhilarating part of her incredible and totally believable life.

So it is, and so it will be.

Love, Marsha

RESTING TO RECEIVE

What you just read is a completely true story. The events were all real. The attention and energy were intense to accomplish it all. It was an example of how inspired action and very necessary inaction (resting to receive) are the conduits to realizing our dreams.

How would you know what inspired action is or what necessary inaction feels like and looks like? When have we been trained or educated about such things? Perhaps a very small percentage of people have ever been guided in these things. Today is the day that guiding begins for you.

INSPIRED ACTION - A GUIDE

Inspired action has many of the following characteristics. It could show up as some of all of these or in additional ways.

- A sense of peace about what you are doing even if it feels a bit scary and uncomfortable.
- There will be a sensation of pulling or tugging, even a lassoed feeling around your solar plexus guiding you gently but specifically in a direction very much toward the new person, place, or thing not away from the old person, place, or thing.
- Leaving or changing a situation will not come with the feeling that what is gone is bad or evil, only that it is no longer suited to your current path.
- You will feel unlocked, physically. Your energy levels seem to be refueled, not depleted, after taking the actions necessary to complete a task.
- Travel days may become super adrenaline-filled. You can lift heavy baggage, last for hours at the airport, and arrive at your destination ready to go out on the town.
- You get an extreme sense of clarity. You KNOW things and you aren't sure how or why. You may never have researched an area, topic, event, etc.; however, you have a sixth sense about it.
- The people or resources you need most arrive almost without any action on your part to find them.
- Even when challenges surface, you meet them with a sense of fascination and wonder, not anger-filled frustration or fear-based procrastination.
- Once things are completed and the desired outcome is achieved, you will look back and marvel with wonder at how things went so smoothly and effortlessly. You will become more aware of what being in flow feels like so that you can better identify that feeling again in the future.

NECESSARY INACTION - A GUIDE

Necessary inaction has many of the following characteristics. It could show up as some of all of these or in additional ways.

- Once you have done certain tasks for the day and you take a step away, put it down completely and don't revisit it until the next day. LET the universe move on your behalf.
- If you have no energy for the things on your to-do list, then take a break. Find a hammock or comfortable spot and LET your mind come up with alternatives. The lack of energy could be a call to rest to allow your higher self sovereignty. IT will give you better solutions to get the job done in a faster and more efficient way.
- Use money as a tool to hire skilled people to help you. It will free your energy. You will learn new things by requesting help OR by training someone to do a task that you don't like to do or perhaps you aren't very proficient at doing. Hiring someone a bit more skilled than you can be well worth the money to get something off your list quickly.
- Enjoying everyday tasks. For example, once I paired my clothing down to a fraction of what I used to have, I actually enjoy doing my laundry. It doesn't stress me out anymore. Having fewer things means I also purchase higher-quality items. I really love those items and how they make me feel, therefore I carefully take care of them.
- Realizing we GET energy from working out. We will not always have the energy we want to have to do the workout initially. Often times we don't "feel like" working out or going for a walk. However, that is the exact thing that will fuel your energy and make you feel better afterward. A reframing message can go a long way such as "I get to work out" versus "I have to work out," or "My body is so strong, and I am proud of it. I work out to keep it moving and strong for my future endeavors."

- Sleeping intentionally. This starts with making up your bed every morning immediately after rising. Don't you always sleep best on a freshly made bed? We spend 1/3 of our lives in bed. It pays to purchase very good bedding. Make sure your bed offers you an amazing sensory experience. Do you love the look and feel of the bed and bedding. How about the smell of the detergent you use to clean the sheets? Do you enjoy the rustle or the crisp sound of the sheets? Have you cut all the tags off the pillows so that they don't irritate you at night so that you can stay asleep once you fall asleep? Does the bed frame squeak or make noises, fix that! Create a very stable, relaxing, comfortable, sexy, and fresh-feeling bed. You will thank yourself in the morning.
- Intentionally create an aesthetically pleasing tea, juice, or coffee routine in the morning. Hunt for a fabulous tea kettle to heat your water. Purchases unique dishes, a gold-toned French press, or a hand-painted coffee carafe. Relax during the preparation and having your drink.

WHERE WE BLOOM

We bloom in the middle of both taking inspired action and receiving intentional rest.

Once you feel the pull of inspired action and answer the call it will shock and amaze you with how much you will complete in a very short amount of time and space.

This is your life. Relish it. Make it feel like the life you want to live. Come back to these lists and observe these characteristics to identify what is happening in your life as often as you need.

Your higher self is giving you permission to bloom!

ABOUT THE AUTHOR

MARSHA GUPTON KING

Marsha Gupton King is currently living in Medellin, Colombia. She is a North Carolina native who raised her two sons in Orlando, Florida.

As an experienced facilitator, she will help guide you back to your joy, bliss, and happiness through mantras, movement, and meditation.

After becoming a certified "Happiness Coach" with Happitude, in collaboration with the Berkeley Well-Being Institute, California, she now offers personal coaching and corporate programs aimed at enhancing the overall happiness and satisfaction of individuals and organizations.

She is an international Kizomba dance instructor and creator of "Zero to Kizomba" which helps new and experienced dancers learn Kizomba in 1-2 hours.

If you are interested in collaborations you can reach her through the following social media channels.

LinkedIn: https://www.linkedin.com/in/marshaguptonking/

Facebook: https://www.facebook.com/marsha.g.king/

Instagram: @kizombalady

WATER PRIESTESS RETURNING HOME

SAMONE MARIE

AS I STEPPED DEEPER INTO THE CORE OF MY SOUL, I
WAS uplifted into a world unlike any I could recall seeing on my
many galactic starseed travels. During these travels, my heart was
the protective vessel to carry me into the portals, my soul the
compass to navigate the remembering of the journey, while my
energetic life force attuned to the vibrational frequency of the
location. I was being summoned to return to what I would later
learn had once been my home.

The voice of this world, calm and enchanting, guided me back
to electric blue waters, as I breathed in the familiar air of my
ancestors once again, feeling the overwhelming sense of freedom I
had been searching for. Sitting on the sandy white beach entranced
by the sight of the waters, without as much as a thought, my
physical human structure was instantly transformed. My massive
cobalt blue wings that had been dormant and energetically hidden
in plain sight for what seemed like ages rose from my shoulder
blades and carried me up into the sky. The feeling of the crisp air

hitting my nostrils as the wind embraced my wings and I soured across the sky. Awwww…I had forgotten my shapeshifting birthright. I had spent so much time in the confines of my Earth-bound body, only escaping through the densities of the Earth by detaching energetically traveling as the pure light energy vessel of my soul.

I could hear the chanting of the ohmmmm ohmmmm ohmmmm calling me as the sound was getting louder and louder. My speed began to pick up in the direction of the sound. Now I could see off in the distance what looked like a glowing land mass. I started to feel a sense of invigoration pour over my body as a light from the land source connected to my heart, much like the one of a lighthouse guiding ships to shore. As I arrived, the massive stone monoliths reached far into the clouds and seemed to form a circle around the landmass that was surrounded by its beautiful electric blue waters. I dove into the water and swam, then emerged to look up to see the monolith of a beautiful mermaid, her tail submerged deep beneath the waters. She and the other monoliths of many other beautiful beings who were chanting the ohmmmm. I could see the sound coming from their mouths and carrying the light to awaken the others.

I was so fascinated by everything that was going on, I hadn't realized that upon hitting the water that my feet were replaced by a fin. I had shapeshifted into a mermaid and the beautiful pastels casting a shimmering glow across my body felt so aligned. Immediately I was greeted by another merwoman who placed a crown on my head adorned with seashells and high-frequency Herkimer diamond crystals. This crown seemed to be held together by energy as it attached to my head. The blue sapphire crystal implanted within my crown chakra many years ago during a shamanic journey began to harmonize with a frequency of light language that seemed to activate something within my being.

She looked at me and said, "Welcome home, we have been anxiously awaiting your arrival. We have so much work to do." With a sense of urgency as she pulled my arm, we went into the depths of the ocean. The next thing I knew I was being called to return to the beach by the calming voice of Shannon Van Den Berg, my publisher whose beautiful shamanic Lemurian activation was guiding me back through my heart and into my body that happen to be physically sitting on my chair in my office of the small apartment I recently moved to in South Florida.

Up until this point, I had truly questioned my connection to Lemuria. Now I felt called to the title and energetics of this book. But didn't know much about Lemuria or had the opportunity to really research it. This all happened so fast—I had so many questions. I would need to return to Lemuria to get the answers to these questions I was seeking. In Shamanism it is our belief that you can return to any moment in time through traveling the spiritual realms by journeying in spirit. This is where you leave behind the densities of your earthbound fleshly body and take flight as pure light, as your soul, to the spiritual realms. I have been on many journeys in my lifetimes, and this experience hit home taking me back to the memories remembering one of my first profound Shamanic journeys back in October of 2014.

JOURNEYING AMONG THE REALMS

I remember the experience like it was yesterday, sitting in the sacred circle with the intention to locate a master teacher within the spirit realm who would give a gift and healing. It is the understanding in Shamanism that we are remembering and that all timelines are simultaneously happening now.

The word Shaman means one who sees in the dark. As the mode of spiritual travel is seeing with your eyes closed. Connecting with the spiritual realms through energetic travel.

Leaving your physical body and teleporting to any given time and location. When you hear the word Shaman, you are usually thinking of the wise elder, a medicine person or an oracle within any given tribe. The 21st century Shamans have been called by the ancestors and awakened to bridge the gap while honoring the ancient practices and amplifying the frequencies of the New Earth.

On this journey I would soon receive my first of many initiations to awakening the Shaman within. Feeling the vibrational beats of the drum took me into an altered state of consciousness. With the intention to connect with my spirit animal, who happens to be a beautiful 12-foot-tall peacock heron. She is absolutely stunning, beautifully adorned with vibrant feathers that have many eyes. She shared a message…

> "We are here to remind you of your wings. The guidance is to look within and shine your bright light to others with love, healing, strength and inner beauty. It is your time to teach the practice of healing from within. Everyone is awaiting your arrival. You are to learn the ways and help heal the world. Return to us daily for guidance, lessons and inner-standing. Speak the truth and follow your intuition. You will gain the friendships and human interactions you desire within this group and many others. You will touch the hearts of many and attract only that which is good for you and your family. Trust yourself, we cannot say that enough. Trust in your own abilities and intuition knowing that you are being directed to do great work. Remember the colors of the peacock feathers and that the eyes symbolize life—giving you the ability to see all that is before, in front, below, behind and above you."

I climbed on her back and we took off to the upper realm. As we transitioned through the portals, there seemed to be a thick, plasmic fog. The upper realm felt familiar and welcoming. I climbed off of her back and sat waiting in what felt like an in-between of some sort.

Before my eyes appeared a huge teepee with smoke rising out the top. I could smell the earthy scent of sage and was drawn in by the sounds of the drums playing vigorously as I felt like I was being summoned. I peered into the tent as if no one could see me, with over 100 people sitting in a sacred circle. The fire in the center crackled and radiated an amber glow. I was mesmerized by the beauty of the woman dancing in the center. She was adorned in a headpiece that looked like a crown made out of beautiful crystals and cream cowrie shells streaming down her face that had a beautiful iridescent glow. Shining bright like glowing stars that shimmer across the night sky. With the swaying of her hips, the beaded skirt made a melody as the seashells clacked together and her arms rolled as she telepathically called to me to join her.

The vibration of the drums proved compelling, enchanting…I felt as if I was in a deep trance as the frequency of my body began to move in ways I never knew possible. We began to move around the circle in a clockwise direction…blowing smoke of sage into the faces of all those in the circle. I moved my hand in a circular motion at the time, not knowing exactly what I was holding…(many years later I would learn that it was my practitioner's crystal singing bowl that divinely chose me after I attended a crystal singing bowl concert in New Mexico). We made our way around the room making sure to connect with everyone. I could feel the love and gratitude radiating within this beautiful space. The deep sense of community and connection was nurturing.

Returning to the center of the circle, she energetically began to pull what looked like a silk scarf from my mouth, releasing all of the negativity, ailments, limitations, pain and worry. She then proceeded to open my head much like opening a jewelry box.

Placing a beautiful blue sapphire at the center, with the gesture of her hand it began to spin, and a crown that had eyes around it emerged from my head.

She said, "You now have the ability to see 360 degrees."

The crown was made of what looked like gold and had the same beautiful colors as the peacock feathers, at the center of each was an eye. She closed my head and sewed it back together. As I could hear the call back the drum began to play, she shared one last message. For me to return to my daily work divining, the knowledge to do it was already within me, and that I was open and ready. She asked that I light a blue candle for her weekly and regain my daily prayers.

At the time I had no clue that I had just received my first priestess initiation with Yemonja. Nor did I know who she was, but felt so divinely connected, loved and supported by her beautiful energy. I also wondered what she had meant by divining. But I would soon discover its meaning and bring more light to her messages.

RECLAIMING MY CROWN

In 2018, on the anniversary of my mother's passing, I embarked on a journey to awaken the water priestess within me and realign with the energy matrix of Yemonja and Olokun. It was a pivotal moment in my life, and I knew I was stepping into my birthright.

During my initiation, I took an oath before God, vowing to honor the sacred IFA oracle while embodying the frequency of Orumila the deity of knowledge, wisdom, and divination. To aid humanity in achieving balance and harmony in life. . My purpose became clear: to be a messenger, weaving the golden threads of spiritual wisdom and bringing them into the light of this physical realm.

Reclaiming My Crown as Iyanifa Ife Tayo, meaning "Love Brings Joy," an IFA Priestess, has been the most transformative journey of my life.

I would spend a year learning the 256 Odus from the sacred Ifa oracle divination system before taking the trip to the retreat center. At the beautiful and majestic Orisa gardens of The Ifa Foundation International in Florida, I spent a week deprogramming from the world and receiving new high-frequency codes of love, joy, peace, health, and wealth. My godparents, Iya Vassa and Philip Neimark, nurtured me with their love and wisdom, and I connected deeply with the energy matrix of the Orisa. I stood before God and vowed to live a life of good character washing away all of my past as I was stepping into the next evolution of my incarnation here on earth that of an Ifa Priestess…a diviner for source (Olodumare) When we open up the sacred IFA portal we are accessing the wisdom and consciousness of all the benevolent beings. Sharing the messages that those are seeking to align and bring balance back into their lives.

As I embrace my initiated name, Iyanifa Ife Tayo, I embody the essence of unconditional love for all.

Prior to receiving my priestess initiation, I merged with the energy matrix of my mother Yemonja and father Olokun Orisa. The Orisa are seen similar to the angels in Western religion. With the attributes of nature as they are said to have once walked the earth. Reminding us of our oneness and connection to Mother Earth.

Yemonja is basically the mother of the fish, as her name comes from the Yoruba words for "mother," "child/children," and "fish." She's all about the sacral chakra, which is in your lower abdomen and deals with creativity, emotions, intuition, and sex. Makes sense that she's often associated with water and the moon, which is a symbol of emotions and creativity.

Then there's Olokun, whose name comes from the Yoruba word for "sea." He's the God of the sea and associated with the throat chakra. That's the one in your neck that controls communication, self-expression, and being honest with yourself and others. Olokun is all about ancient knowledge and wisdom, which totally fits with the deep ocean vibes and the planet Neptune. It's said that he can help you find your voice and speak your truth…while bringing you all the world's riches…as the bottom of the ocean is known to be the place of lost shipwrecks, lives and buried treasures.

UNDERSTANDING MY GIFTS

When I aligned myself with the energetics of my birthright, I awakened the "LIT AS FUCK" Water Priestess… with the ability to amplify the frequency of those around me. Harnessing my power of creativity and maternal love activated by my heart and ignited through the deeply rooted portal within my womb. Reconnecting with ancient wisdom, honoring and sharing practices and rituals. Water is a powerful tool that I learned to utilize, as it is programmable and makes up most of our bodies and the planet. With my gift, I empower others to awaken their own abilities to program the water from within and merge it with energies of vitality, abundance, peace, and joy. Through simple practical and actionable tools, resources, and modalities. In my signature program, "Unfuck Yourself Soul Emersion Retreat," I share the ancient teachings of how to imbue water with these energies for a transformative experience.

People often ask me what's the secret to the work that I do with my clients? It's knowing that reconnecting to your heart amplifies its vibrational frequency of the universal language of unconditional love, empowering you to realign to your soul's purpose through the connection of your ancestors, spirit guides, source and speaking life into your mind, body and soul is the key to reclaiming your life.

I invite you to connect with the loving and fertile energy matrix of my mother Orisa Yemonja and the protective and abundant energy of my father Olokun through this beautiful activation. Inspired by a prayer written by my godmother Iya Vassa, let us tap into the wisdom and power of the Orisa together.

Begin your activation by finding a quiet and comfortable place where you will not be disturbed.

> Take a deep breath in through your nose, hold it for a moment, and then release it slowly with a deep sigh through your mouth.

> Take another deep breath in through your nose, hold it for a moment, and then release it slowly with a deep sigh through your mouth.

> Repeat this a few times until you feel yourself becoming more relaxed.

> As you continue to breathe deeply, focus your attention on the flow of the beautiful tranquil waters connecting with the energy of Yemonja/Olokun. Allow the words to resonate within you, feeling the gratitude for all that supports you today.

> Now, bring your attention to your intention to align your energy with the unique energy matrix of Yemonja/Olokun. Visualize a path opening up before you, leading you to the ocean and greater opportunities to connect with this

expansive energy.

As you continue to breathe deeply, allow yourself to become fully immersed in this energy field. Feel yourself staying afloat as you travel each day of life, with your thoughts fluid and in movement.

Visualize yourself tapping into your inner knowledge, seeing the light inside your beautiful heart, bringing light even in the deep dark places. Allow the coolness of water to wash away any negative thoughts, purifying your mind and soul.

Allow yourself to be receptive to the messages that come through the sounds of life's crashing waves, guiding you to your destiny. Visualize yourself becoming stabilized even when things are rough, able to take in replenishing energy and remove that which is not good for you.

Finally, see yourself knowing your safe space, protecting yourself and those you love. Repeat the words "Yemonja ahh sesu...ahh sesu Yemonja Yemonja o lodo, oloda Yemonja Asè" as a final affirmation of your connection with this energy matrix.

Take a deep breath in and slowly exhale, feeling a sense of peace and serenity. When you are ready, slowly open your eyes and return to the present moment, carrying with you the energy of Yemonja/Olokun throughout your day.

As you return to your physical body, I invite you to take a few moments to reflect on your experience:

What did you feel during the activation?

What messages or insights did you receive?

How can you continue to connect with the energy of Yemonja and Olokun to empower your life?

Journal about your experience and any thoughts or feelings that came up for you. Remember, the Orisa are always with us, guiding us on our journey if we open ourselves up to their wisdom and power.

I invite you to journey with me. Let's dive into the depths of your soul and emerge as the beautiful, free, and abundant being that you were meant to be.

ABOUT THE AUTHOR

SAMONE MARIE

Samone Marie is the founder of Soulestial Comm-UNITY, a transformative journey that combines practical tools, ancestral wisdom, and a heart-centered supportive community. With her guidance, you'll release self-limiting thought patterns and activate your heart and soul, allowing you to discover inner peace, embrace love, and find joy in everyday living.

As a Soulestial Guide, Ancestral Medium, Mindset Facilitator, and 7-time International Bestselling Author, Samone Marie's work is grounded in the ancient wisdom of the ancestors and amplified by the unconditional love that lives within her heart and deeply rooted within the womb embodied by her initiated frequency of Yemonja(Yeh Mow Jaa), the Yoruban goddess of the oceans. You can say she's a modern day water priestess. Through channeling benevolent spirit guides and illuminating the channeled ancient wisdom of the Ancestors and Source, she aims to raise the consciousness of humanity and activate 21st-century medicine within the hearts of those she works with.

Samone Marie's passion for mindfulness and well-being is evident in her offerings of children's yoga and facilitation of the mindset programs, retreats and workshops. However, her upcoming book, Soulestial: Starseeds Awakened Through The Ancient Wisdom Of Their Ancestors, is set to be released in late fall and will be the centerpiece of her work. This transformative journey towards deeper alignment with your ancient origin will be a guide for those seeking to unlock their full potential.

An Oregon Native, Samone Marie followed her soul's calling and love for the ocean and now resides in South Florida with her husband and twin sons. Her emphasis on Soulestial Comm-UNITY reflects her dedication to creating a community of individuals seeking to awaken their souls and live their best lives. Let Samone Marie guide and support you on your journey towards reclaiming your life and unlocking your full potential.

Begin the journey to reclaiming the power within here: https://www.samonemarie.com/

AMBASSADORS OF THE HEART

SHANNON VAN DEN BERG

I BREATHED IN A RAGGED BREATH. MY EYES CLOSED, TRYING TO CENTER MYSELF. I felt the cool, coarse sand under my bare feet and the moist breeze blow my silky dress against my skin. I heard the waves crashing, and then sizzling as they raced upon the shore and then back again.

I opened my eyes and looked out across the horizon where Mama Pacific met the sky as my heart ached. My body wanted to crumble to the ground like a child allows itself to do, feeling the agony of extreme loss.

I remembered this as one of my past lives in Lemuria. I was a priestess of Lemuria who chose to stay behind after one of the destruction cycles where Lemurian civilization regenerated itself as most civilizations did. I did this out of divine service to humanity to anchor the frequencies of Lemuria on the planet because it was needed, then, as it's needed now.

Having to say goodbye to my beloved paradise, community

and every thing I loved so dearly was almost more than I could bear. My heart felt like it was being wrenched out of my body, but my devotion kept me standing, kept me holding on to the next expression of Lemuria I had stayed to help birth.

This is what I experienced and felt during my first shamanic journey over 25 years ago and one of my deepest woundings. The loss and abandonment. The feeling of lost ecstasy, loss of my brothers and sisters. The lost heaven on earth I think we all still long for deep in our souls today.

For those of us, the starseeds, volunteers, light warriors and emissaries of the Golden Age, who've volunteered to be here at this unprecedented time on our planet, I believe we all feel this kind of loss on some level. I believe this is one of the reasons we don't tap into these ancient rememberings, because the loss of this and other mother civilization is excruciatingly painful.

So just like my unwavering commitment to stay behind and guide humanity forward before, I invite you to remember with me.

It's time we remember the feeling of what it was like to live in an exquisite and abundant mother civilization like Lumeria. Where we were so deeply connected to Pachamama, each other, and everything around us.

It's time we remember the way forward.

COMING HOME

I've been an ambassador of the heart all my life, but never experienced a deeper heart awakening than on a recent trip to Kauai, Hawaii, where the echoes of Lemuria are loud.

I grew up on the southern Californian shores of Mama Pacific but chose to follow the divine breadcrumbs to Colorado where I've grown a family, homesteaded and stewarded the land for 26 years.

I'd held myself away from the ocean and many chances to visit Hawaii for too long - the painful memories kept me inland.

This last winter when my third son turned 21, we took a family trip to Kauai to celebrate. I have been activated by land, and I activate land as a grid worker, but never have I had the depth of homecoming like I did when we landed in Lihue.

I walked into the open air airport and felt my heart open wider. I took in the feeling of walking into a living breathing temple. I felt the aliveness of the wind, humidity, and the deep sacredness of a land. A land that felt as ancient as Lemuria with her ancestors, stewards, plants, animals, the waters and land itself all expressed in beauty and love.

Kauai has this nourishing grandmother energy that reaches out to embrace you. It is like going home after you've been away for a long time, and having those waiting arms of family to fall into. Every plant on the island from the sacred ferns to Hibiscus to Lokelani roses radiated tangible energy, the sound of the rain and swaying palms let me sink deeper into it all, the plentiful, continuous crowing roosters keep bringing you back to the present moment with every crow, and the ocean, well, She sang me back to myself one wave at a time.

My body responded to the rapture of being on this sacred island with my chronic body pain vanishing. My youngest son and I both felt transformed by just being there - for 2 people with nervous system disorders, it was a speedy and miraculous realignment to normal. It was the greatest homecoming I've experienced this lifetime. There is no place in the world like it, surrounded by magical waters, it is a living piece of Lemuria and felt like I was finally home.

This feeling of home, this rootedness changed me. I felt deeply,

deeply nourished. This nourishment wasn't in a I'm trying to nourish myself kind of way, but in the natural dynamic of being gifted nourishment from overflow. This freely gifted overflow flooded my body, reminding me of our capacity to trust and receive freely. I communed with Grandmother Kauai and Mama Pacific in a heart practice, every day. My heart kept expanding, and my oneness with all things deepened. I realized my next chapter had begun, my new timeline had merged into reality.

I've been a medicine women and feminine leadership pioneer for over 2 decades, owned herbal stores, created a healing center and practice, own a potent boutique publishing company I have reinvented the wheel with, where over 200 women have become published authors with me, I am devoted to my growth and leading the way for frequency leaders. I am always evolving in service to the collected, and this homecoming brought landslides of medicine for our time through to be expressed, I felt an elevated level of embodying an ambassador of the heart unfolding within me.

I flew home to Colorado with my family, but in my heart, Kauai is home. Not only were our family trip pictures put up on the walls of our living room, but pictures of ferns, Lokelani roses, Mama Pacific with the moon shining on Her and the shores of Kauai where the ocean meets the land went up as soon as we got home.

I started learning the Hawaiian language, reading Hawaiian mythology and history, and working with fern medicine and Ke'oni Hanalei, a contemporary wisdom keeper of Mu. All as this book, Priestess of Lemuria, was being created.

I realized that deep seated feeling of home is a fresh, uncharted, hugely overlooked portal to who we BE. It takes everything, and I mean everything to a new level of clarity and tapped-in-ness. It's like a second spiritual awakening really. To be able to truly come home to yourself, your temporary pin point on the planet, your medicine, your soul work - it's like seeing it all for the first time. Seeing it through the lens of the heart.

THE WAY OF THE HEART

Living the way of the heart is creating the new Lemuria in our current timelines.

The collective is shifting, more and more of us are dearmoring, expanding and relearning to live the way of the heart. As the heart openings and awakenings become more our way of being, running that energy through all we do and all we are, this consciousness will expand through us and out across time and space. That's when the Golden Age will land.

Living from the heart is a frequency, an intelligence, a consciousness. a connection between our body temple and our soul, and a channel for the infinite power of love.

Heart-centered beingness is the liminal space that transcends all.

The truth of this can be seen in how you handle conflict. If there is a disagreement and you go to your heart, you will easefully find a loving and beneficial solution for everyone. I've experienced this time and time again, where the second I step into an argument that is about to go sideways, both parties soften, then gain clarity and empathy. Before they know it, they are lowering their symbolic weapons of anger and guarding themselves. They are able to stay open and true to themselves and each other, while coming to a very different conclusion.

Imagine this kind of power in our world today.

This is not what we are taught in our society. We are taught to be in our heart-centeredness is weak and unrealistic, which ties to the feminine being the same, since women are naturally associated with this consciousness. I love that in Hawaiian shamanism, the heart center or the 'Uhane (oo ha-nee) is associated with the masculine which changes this whole narrative!

What if being so deeply rooted in our heart was part of our divine power? It is!

Our Lemurian ancestors and those still guiding us from beyond this realm through the Agartha network and Telos in Mt. Shasha, left a legacy of love for us to get our bearings in these times and truly create a heaven on earth matrix now.

Here 3 access points for you to bring more of this heart medicine into your beingness.

FOUNDATIONS OF FREQUENCY

Frequency was the main current of Lemurian civilization, and the frequency of the heart was the thread that pierced every part of beingness of this time. Intention, prayers, ceremony, love, communication, healing, all of it was based in heart-centered frequency.

Everything from leadership to birth to building to travel, every part of life was about frequency.

Lemurian leaders held this heart frequency. In Lemuria there was no hierarchy, to be a leader was a great honor and power was sacred. Leaders led with compassion, truth, balance, and interconnectedness.

The Lemurian Elder Council was the epitome of embodied wisdom and upheld the sovereignty of all with grace. That same grace and wisdom can be called on today to transcend the Great Reset and find our path to the next Golden Age.

Every Lemurian held this frequency of the heart. Mothers and fathers were revered as guides and honored for going through the process of giving and nurturing life. They were not alone, children were held as precious beings, gods and goddesses in form by the entire community. The whole saying that it takes a village to raise a child, originated with the Lemurians. The children belonged to everyone in the community, the waters and the planet Herself. We belonged to each other, everything was a weaving of this heart frequency.

Frequency healing was an art. Sound and frequency were innerstood at high, masterful levels. The lands and waters, animals and plants danced with us and within us to bring pleasure, bliss, joy, and vitality into life.

Everything is frequency now just as it was then, we are just taught otherwise. Lemurians knew this and embodied the care and tending, creation and balance of frequency as utmost importance.

In Lemuria the oceans and waters were revered and respected as sacred conduits of frequency. Our star family emissaries, the dolphins and whales infused cosmic codes into the oceans through their songs and sounds. Just as our star families infused energy into the land and water tables like we see now in the UK crop circles. These frequencies then rippled through the land and entire planet.

Water has ancient origins and mystical properties. It holds frequency, takes on attunement, and then affects other frequencies. It carries memories, is ever changing in form and cycle, and makes up the majority of our own bodies.

How can we not be affected by frequency?

The women in this book are water priestesses because we innerstand the magic and importance of water in carrying frequency and expanding heart consciousness. We speak our

156

prayers and intentions into the water we drink, we make offerings and sing to rivers, oceans and waterfalls, and hold ceremonies with water.

Water and frequency can be easily accessed by everyone. The acknowledgement, respect, belief and surrender is where we come into relationship and playful exploration of them.

ALL OUR RELATIONS

If everything is frequency, then everything is one. Our Lemurian brothers and sisters lived and breathed this truth. Relationships are heart medicine. We must heal, integrate and open ourselves to be able to connect to something beyond us. Respect, love and connections flow effortlessly in this frequency.

In Lemuria,relationship was part of their deeply held belief in the interconnectedness of all. Holding this brought forth the rightness of how they lived, cooperative and co-creative collaboration, and a true heartfelt desire to serve the collective.

When I first felt into this concept, I had so much conditioning that there is either the individual good or the collective good, but definitely not both. So then, how do we choose?

In Lemuria there was only both - the personal and collective thriving because of one another. Iit was not a concession on either part. It was a real, wholehearted community working in aligned vision and values. These are the types of deep dives I like to explore and be able to try on, and then anchor as a new frequency.

When we hold the attitude of love, the prospect of community changes. No longer do we co-inhabit, but co-create. We don't guard and exclude, but feel into ways to contribute and support each other.

Partnerships thrive when both people are whole and bring all of themselves to mutually loving relationships. Raising, guiding and teaching our children becomes a natural priority. Elders are honored as pillars of the community for the wisdom and frequency masters they are.

I was raised by my grandparents which has always given me a different perspective on relationships, especially how disconnected we are as a society. I noticed how our greater community excludes and lacks a place for its elders and children. And the severing force of competitive drive to out do each other and isolate to ensure no overlap in energy.

The house I grew up in was a shrine to this isolation and my grandparent's 1950's keeping-up-with-the-jones mentality. I felt it viscerally through the wrought iron fences adorned with pointy tips at the tops, and cinder block walls you couldn't see over keeping the world out.

It's made me take notice of all the ways we can choose connection, from helping a mom with a screaming baby in line at the grocery store, to taking a moment to look someone in the eyes and ask sincerely how they are doing, then listen intently to the response, to healing the relationship within ourselves and close relationships.

I feel we overlook the point at which we move forward into connection and then greater interconnectiveness, or step back into those isolating cultural norms.

In Lemuria interconnectedness extended way beyond how they treated their fellow humans, star family and soul guides. It encompassed the animals, plants, waters, and every facet of Pachamama. The respect, the love, the collaboration, everything I talked about before was extended to all. And they all responded as the intricate web of life they were treated as. The Earth held us in return.

Many see our beautiful planet as an inanimate object, that's how we got in the mess we're in today. They don't feel Her as some of us do. They don't value the feminine or the mother. They don't understand the limited capacity She is running at. Just as I realized with 3 babies under the age of three, mamas are miraculous but we need cared for too. Pachamama, our mother is no different, she needs us to listen, to work with Her, to heal Her, to let Her help us.

When we sync our bodies and hearts with Pachamama, give Her offerings, learn and communicate with Her, we open to a relationship with Her.

Opening to plants, animals, crystals and trees is one of the ways we can connect with Pachamama and learn this forgotten interconnected way of being.

When we allow our heart to open to the plants and give them permission to work with us, they have so much to teach us. I often have people ask me why plant medicine works the way it does for me, it's because I've cultivated a relationship with the plants. I've opened myself to them. I listened to them on all levels and my heart is open to them. I come to them not to fix something or to right something but to have their counsel, to engage with their frequency, to merge their wisdom with my intention, together we move in a dance.

Everytime we place our intentional focus on our relations and connecting, we start to move into a new paradigm of true community.

DIVINE CONTRIBUTION

The way of the heart was intriguingly connected to

contribution in Lemuria.

Every person had respect and responsibility for themselves and their community, a frequency standard of who they were. Every person worked to be their most authentic self, their highest self, their most healed self, to contribute that frequency to the whole and beyond.

Within this is the truth that each of us is inherently worthy. We all have something, many things, to contribute. Our unique personality, talents, and frequency are of huge value just as they are.

Take that in for a moment.

I believe this is one of the biggest downfalls of our society, is the lack of people feeling like they have something to contribute. This breeds disconnection because they're not putting energy in the reciprocity cycle, then are not naturally resourced from that cycle.

Life is a dynamic flow of give and receive. When we do either, the other is a natural result. So if people feel there is nothing to give and don't naturally receive, that leaves us with the toxic, overbearing taking of things, to the extreme of that being without consent.

In Lemurian communities there was a place for everyone and their gifts. There were elders, people that were further along the path than you who were frequency masters. There were your colleagues, those who walked along the path with you, and your juniors who were those either starting on the journey or quite a few steps behind you. Each position was a contribution to the other's.

Can you imagine a community that was based on expression and your unique beingness as contribution?

A community that had space and purpose for everyone?

For me contribution looks a lot like following our own heart medicine, what we love, what we're naturally good at, what comes through us.

Contribution at its highest form is the embodiment of becoming the vessel for the divine. Surrendering to becoming the channel and trusting our own expression of it.

My contribution to humanity is being a beacon of unconditional love and heart consciousness.

Carrying this Lemurian heart frequency as a sacred disruptor here to awaken and hold space for New Earth leaders to rise, my brothers, sisters and children included.

Being a mother, guiding and schooling my children.

The plants I commune with, tend, eat and make medicine with.

The ceremonies I hold, offerings I make, and relations and spirits I work with.

Choosing to homestead, live slowly and in sync with the seasons.

My great love for and connection with Pachamama and Her waters.

Cooking nourishing meals from scratch and infusing food with healing and prayers.

My depth, tenacity and urgency to expand my consciousness and trailblaze the way for others.

Stewarding and singing to the land.

Loving so deeply it cracks people open.

All of it is contribution and all of it is equal, it is my beingness that is the offering, the divine contribution.

After many years of teaching expression and storytelling, I've learned we are heavily conditioned to contribution having a specific and tangible result. However this is not true. When we limit the range of results, we leave out the magic, possibility and artistry.

When contribution becomes a collaboration with God, Pachamama, and our heart, it has infinite expressions and is soul-full.

Play and curiosity are the antidotes to contribution not being pure and potent, for it staying out of the head and relieved of judged results.

When we can express and contribute as fully as we can in any given moment, it changes our frequency, amplifying and setting it ablaze with life force. Resourcing it with more energy, we are then able to deepen that expressive contribution, perpetuating the magnification of impact and reach.

When people talk about flow state or creative flow, this is what they are referring to. It's a completely normal state of trust and divine co-creation that will change our world immeasurably once more of us can embody that frequency.

The gift of being and expressing your entire soul self, the sum and beautiful integration of all of your lifetimes, relations, ancestors and lineages, is the biggest magic you can bring forward for humanity. You can then learn to share yourself and express yourself to the extent you offer your frequency in attunement and communion with your brothers and sisters.

PRIESTESS OF LEMURIA SPEAKS

Sister, come partake of the rememberings of heaven on earth.

The feelings that will move you into the divine dance of the ages.

The sacred becoming.

The rightness in every facet of being.

A deep belonging that can be felt in your bones.

The beauty in a reality that originates from the heart.

The interconnectedness of planet, people, animals, plants and cosmos.

Souls abundantly expressed and acknowledged.

Hearts in union.

Pachamama holding us as the Divine Mother.

Wrapping Her nourishing elements and energies around us.

Our hearts synced to Her cycles, memory and shifts.

Effortlessly moving between form and spirit.

The great weaving of the ages.

The divinity and depth within.

New Lemuria emerges.

AMBASSADORS STEP FORWARD

I've witnessed more and more light leaders stepping forward in the last 30 years. Most take a few steps and then stop, so much in the way of their path.

The pain of loss and abandonment they may not even know is there, stopping them in their tracks.

Not quite feeling at home on this planet or even that they want to be here.

Dabbling in their soul work, but still hiding their bigger magic.

Feeling unsatisfied or restless, bottled up expression waiting to be spent.

Holding themselves inexplicably away from the true birth they are so ready for.

And my heart breaks. It breaks for the light leaders, the planet and all who are praying for them to step forward.

If this is you, invite you to take another step.

To step into the medicine of your own heart.

As a water priestess, I work with water in many ways. One of my favorite ways to work with water is coding water.

It's a simple ritual to infuse frequency into your water, ask for the water to work with you, and then ingest the water letting it merge with your being and you to be attuned to that frequency by it.

Try it. It's a powerful way to work with water that takes a few moments of intention.

Grab a glass of water (glass preferably!).

Land for a moment with your right hand over your heart and your left hand over your sacral.

Take a deep breath.

Hold the glass close to your month and speak or sing to the water:

Heart opening. Abundance. Joy. Courage. (What you are desiring to attune to)

I ask the waters to bless the waters of my body.

I ask the waters to bless the waters of this planet.

I ask the waters to bless the waters of our galaxy.

I ask the waters to bless the waters of the Universe. (And/or, you can say your star lineage here, example: I ask the water to bless the waters of Sirius).

Thank you, thank you, thank you.

Amen. Aho. So it is. Aloha ma.

I code my water and teas multiple times a day. I find some people who do this don't feel the water shift right away, but oftentimes notice subtle changes in how they feel first.

Water, frequency, cultivating relationships and community, and your divine contribution are all ways to connect to this unfurling beautiful and important energy of Lemuria.

These bring you deeper into yourself where you can remember who you are and why you're here. Then you can feel the authentic movement of how you desire to express that into the world.

This is what I do. I activate frequency leaders into deeper levels of leadership, expression and BEing from the heart. After I wrote this, I channeled through a transmission on New Lemuria and how to engage with Lemurian frequency for you. You can access the complimentary transmission through my Work with Me Link at the conclusion of my About the Author and Publisher page which follows.

I'd like to invite you to let me know what landed for you in this chapter. You can email me at Shannon@shannonvandenberg.com.

Thank you for remembering with me.

Thank you for being an ambassador of the heart.

Aloha ma.

ABOUT THE AUTHOR & PUBLISHER

SHANNON VAN DEN BERG

Shannon Van Den Berg is the CEO of Kiva Publishing, International Bestseller 10 times over, and Feminine Leadership Pioneer for over two decades.

She activates New Earth feminine leaders into their next level embodiment and expression through blazing the trail for the sacred art of feminine leadership during the Great Shift. She believes humanity needs your medicine and is here to support you in sharing your story and message with the world.

She holds space for her sisters to rise through her powerful collaborative books, activation portals, her Quantum Creatrix

Oracle Deck and revolutionary Jaguar Leadership Council for fierce feminine frequency leaders.

Her upcoming portal, Coming Home: The Heart of Lemurian Leadership was created to bring feminine starseeds, visionaries and light leaders into ownership of their soul mission with the clarity and confidence to lead themselves and their community from grounded embodiment.

She lives on her homestead in the sacred Four Corners area of Hesperus, Colorado with her husband and four homeschooled boys.

If you feel pulled to dive deeper into Lemurian leadership codes, join her in the Coming Home portal through the link below, or send her a message to find the right fit for you to take your next steps.

Work with me: https://linktr.ee/shannonvandenberg_%5C

Connect with me on Tiktok: https://www.tiktok.com/@shannonvandenberg_

Follow Me on Instagram: https://www.instagram.com/shannonvandenberg_/

Friend me on Facebook: https://www.facebook.com/shannonlvandenberg

Printed in Great Britain
by Amazon

45276604R00099